The Purpose-Driven Principal

FINDING FOCUS IN THE CHAOS OF
SCHOOL LEADERSHIP

Michelle Sloan

PRINCIPAL PRINCIPLES PUBLICATIONS

Author/MICHELLE SLOAN
msloan@sloanleadership.com
https://sloanleadership.com

Book Layout ©2017 BookDesignTemplates.com

Ordering Information:
Quantity sales. Special discounts are available on quantity purchases by corporations, associations, and others. For details, contact the "Special Sales Department" at the email address above.

The Purpose-Driven Principal/ Michelle Sloan —1st ed.
ISBN 979-8-9987351-2-7 (Paperback)
ISBN 979-8-9987351-3-4 (Hardback)
ISBN 979-8-9987351-4-1 (eBook)

Table of Contents

Praise for The Purpose-Driven Principal

"The Purpose-Driven Principal is a powerful and timely resource for today's school leaders. Michelle masterfully weaves personal experience and practical insight to show why purpose must remain the foundation of effective leadership. Grounded in the pillars of people, pedagogy, process, and professional development, this book offers a clear framework for building strong, sustainable leadership. A must-read for every new principal committed to leading with clarity, courage, and purpose."

— *Dr. Brandi Kelly, Speaker,* author, and founder of Spark HOPE Edu

"Michelle Sloan's The Purpose Driven Principal is a must-read for every school leader who has ever felt the tension between their vision and the daily realities of the job. With refreshing vulnerability and honesty, Michelle invites readers into her own journey—sharing both the missteps and the meaningful breakthroughs that shaped her leadership. Her writing feels like a conversation with a trusted mentor: authentic, encouraging, and deeply practical. Whether you are a new principal finding your footing or a seasoned leader seeking renewal, The Purpose Driven Principal will remind you why you chose this work—and how to lead with heart, clarity, and confidence."

—*Dr. Ashlee Boothe,* author, and owner, AB Consulting

"In The Purpose-Driven Principal, Michelle has captured what it feels like to be overwhelmed by the responsibility of leading a school. Through her personal stories and experiences, she connects directly with readers and provides a clear framework for a manageable path forward. She's masterfully captured her coaching conversations on the pages of the book, cheering you on, asking questions, posing possibilities, and describing practical applications. We wished we would have had this book much earlier in our careers!"

—*Kurtis and Lorna Hewson,* authors of the best-selling book *Collaborative Response: Three Foundational Components That Transform How We Respond to the Needs of Learners*

i

"As someone obsessed with sustainable systems, this book had me screaming, "YES!" Michelle brilliantly translates the overwhelming "purpose" into a practical, repeatable "how." She nails the fact that leadership isn't about having all the answers; it's about building the systems (like her "Brain Binders" and "Assess-Design-Align" cycle) that create clarity and stop the constant-crisis-mode. This book is the guide every overwhelmed school leader is desperately craving."

—*Jessica Lane,* Director of Integration and Analytics at Symplifyed

"You know how some school leaders seem to enjoy their jobs while so many don't? Here's their secret: They've aligned their purpose with the actual work. And this book shows you exactly how to do it."

—*Danny Bauer,* Chief Ruckus Maker, author, podcast host, and international speaker.

"Being a leader can feel overwhelming. There are so many resources out there, yet not enough time to even know where to start. If this is the case for you, this book is exactly the right place to begin. It's written from personal experience, which is both affirming and encouraging, but also stays grounded in research and best practice. You'll feel like you're pulling up a coach right alongside you as you read this book! "

—*Casey Watts,* speaker, author of *The Craft of Clarity*

"In a world where principals are pulled in every direction, Michelle Sloan offers a framework that brings leadership back to its true center—purpose. The Purpose Driven Principal is more than a leadership manual; it's a blueprint for sustainable culture. Michelle writes with the empathy of someone who's been in the seat, the clarity of a strategist, and the conviction of a leader who knows that culture begins and ends with people. Her four pillars—People, Pedagogy, Processes, and Professional Growth—translate the complexity of school leadership into actionable rhythms that build trust, focus, and joy. Every educator who wants to lead with intention, not exhaustion, should read this book."

— *Dr. Chris Owen*, Culture Coach & Founder, OwenCo Solutions

Dedication

To every principal who wakes up each day determined to make a difference.

To those just beginning the journey, finding their footing and discovering their voice.

To those in the thick of it, carrying the weight and showing up anyway.

To those who've finished the race, whose legacy lives on in the leaders and students they shaped.

You have one of the hardest jobs in education. You lead with courage when no one sees. You make impossible decisions with incomplete information. You carry the dreams of students, the hopes of families, and the weight of a community.

This book is for you.

Acknowledgements

I never planned to write a book. But the more I worked with principals, the more I realized we're all learning the same lessons, often the hard way. I started thinking about the frameworks and approaches that turned things around for me and for the schools I've coached. If these ideas made leadership more transparent and more sustainable for me, they could help others, too.

Being a principal is one of the most challenging jobs I've ever done, and also one of the most rewarding. It's demanding because so many rely on the principal for support, guidance, and direction, students who need a safe and positive place to learn, teachers who look for encouragement and stability, parents who seek partnership and trust, and a community that holds high expectations for the future. Communities that expect from them. Initiatives that never stop coming. Being a principal is one of the most challenging jobs I've ever done, and also one of the most rewarding.

I'm grateful to the many people who made this book and this journey possible.

To my husband, Sean, who has been my greatest supporter in writing this book and in life. You walked through neighborhoods beside me while I listened to podcasts, processing ideas out loud. You sat with me on long drives as I absorbed the audiobooks that shaped my thinking. You made countless dinners while I stayed up writing long past bedtime. You never stopped believing in this work or in me.

To my mom and my sister, who celebrate every win and share my work with others. Your support means the world to me.

To my sons, teaching you to read remains one of my proudest achievements. Thank you for the countless ways you've supported my career over the years, from attending summer camps where I worked to helping with projects and volunteering at school events. You've sacrificed time with me so I could serve others, and I'm grateful. Being your mom is my greatest privilege.

To the teachers and staff I worked with in my early years as a principal, I owe you a big apology. I had no idea what I was doing. Like, zero clue. Nobody prepares you for this job, and I'm pretty sure I proved that daily. But somehow you gave me grace and patience. We did have a ton of fun together, though! Thank you for your honest feedback. I'm a better leader because of you.

To those who saw something in me before I believed in myself and gave me opportunities to lead, thank you for your trust and belief in me.

To my pastor, for teaching me about leading people and how to carry the weight of leadership.

To Dhustie, my lifelong friend. You've cleaned lockers, attended my school fundraisers, supported my business, sorted files, prayed for me, and helped me make tough decisions in life. You're my ride or die, my wild and crazy friend, and I'm so grateful for you.

To Stephanie, for giving me the opportunity to write this book.

To June and Virginia, for leading alongside me, encouraging me when the work felt heavy, and supporting me through every challenge.

To Ruth, who saw potential in me in my early years and helped develop the leader in me.

To Danny, a master storyteller and brutally honest coach, who encouraged me to be myself and step out of my comfort zone.

And to every principal I've had the privilege to coach: thank you for trusting me with your challenges, your dreams, and your growth. You inspire me every single day.

And to my Lord and Savior, Jesus Christ, through whom all things are possible.

This book exists because of all of you.

The Purpose Driven
Principal Framework

People

Pedagogy

Processes

Professional
Growth

Assess ⟶ Design ⟶ Align

Purpose

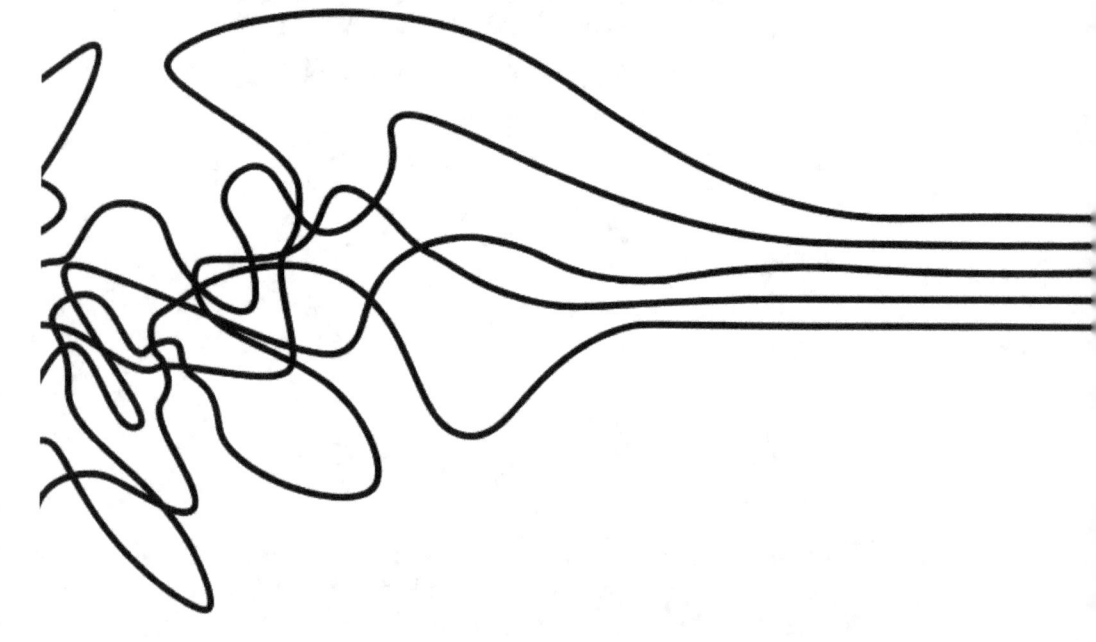

Where Purpose Begins

When I first stepped into the principal's role, I thought I was ready. I dreamed about shaping a positive culture, building strong relationships, and helping kids become the best version of themselves. But reality hit me fast. Nobody prepared me to manage a multi-million dollar budget, handle difficult parent conversations, or even put together a master schedule. My days were crammed with paperwork, discipline issues, and back-to-back meetings. Most nights, I went home wondering if I was doing anything right. I felt like I was making mistake after mistake because I was so rushed.

If you've led a school for any length of time, you know that feeling. The weight of responsibility. The never-ending to-do list. The way you're pulled away from the very things that made you want to lead in the first place.

> **You still care deeply, but caring doesn't fix the chaos.**

You still care deeply, but caring doesn't fix the chaos.

It took me years to figure out how to move beyond the cycle of reacting to chaos. I read books, listened to podcasts, and sat in countless conversations with mentors and colleagues. I tried new strategies, failed, got back up, and kept going. Some days, it felt like trial and error was the only leadership plan I had. And after enough late nights and too many days of spinning my wheels, I finally got fed up. I was investing energy into countless tasks that didn't matter, but never getting to the heart of why I became a principal in the first place. If I were going to build the kind of school I had always dreamed of, then I knew something had to change.

Little by little, I began leading differently. I stopped trying to do everything that came across my desk and started implementing simple systems so the important work could actually happen. I learned to step back and ask hard questions about what mattered and what didn't. It wasn't quick or perfect, but over time, the weight started to lift. I wasn't just reacting to unexpected situations; I started proactively building capacity in my schedule for building my vision. I found joy again, and I began to lead the way I had always hoped I could.

Today, I get to walk alongside principals who are where I once was. Through coaching, leadership cohorts, and practical tools, I support new leaders in finding their footing and experienced leaders ready for a hard reset. I've watched schools move from barely surviving to making progress and even thriving. I've seen leaders on the verge of quitting discover hope, confidence, and a renewed sense of purpose.

That's why I wrote this book. Not to hand you another checklist or overwhelm you with more work. My goal is to help you reconnect with your purpose, reignite your passion, and establish practical systems that empower you to lead with joy.

Schools are complex, with different personalities, cultures, beliefs, and needs in every classroom and home. That's why we'll keep coming back to purpose and be intentional with the Four Pillars: build strong relationships (People), define and support great teaching and learning (Pedagogy), put simple, repeatable structures in place (Processes), and keep growing ourselves and our teams (Professional Growth). The goal isn't perfection; it's steady progress by getting a little better every day.

In the pages ahead, we'll define Purpose as the foundation for school leadership. Then we'll walk through the Four Pillars of a purpose-driven school: People, Pedagogy, Processes, and Professional Growth. Finally, we will introduce the Assess–Design–Align cycle, a specific, continuous three-step cycle you will use to objectively measure the health of each Pillar, pinpoint specific weaknesses, and implement targeted changes to secure long-term results.

You'll hear my personal stories and experiences. I'll share my wins, mistakes, and everything in between, as well as stories from leaders I've coached. You'll find strategies you can implement right away, not to give you more to do, but to help you make the most out of your time and be intentional about developing a thriving, purpose-driven school.

By the time you finish this book, I hope you'll feel renewed. I want you to rediscover the joy of leadership and walk your halls with confidence, knowing you are leading on purpose and through your purpose. Your students and staff need you. Your community needs you. Our future needs you. You have a purpose and a calling that only you can fulfill.

That purpose is still waiting for you.

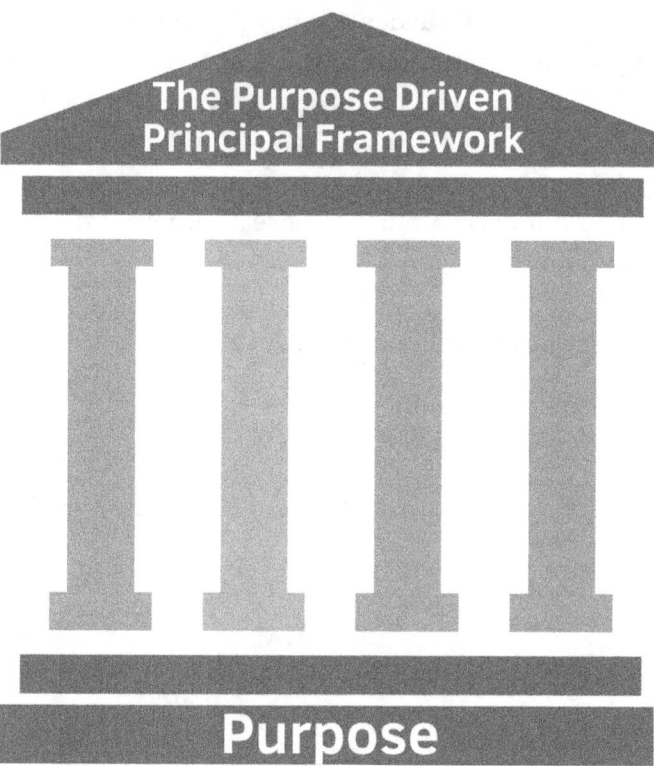

CHAPTER 1

Building the Foundation

My first day leading a new school began with sirens in the rearview mirror.

It was July 2020, my seventh year as a principal and my first week in a new state, stepping into a new school as principal in the middle of a pandemic. That morning was meant for my final prep for our Meet and Greet and my first chance to meet my new staff. I was filled with anticipation and expectations of arriving early with plenty of time to prepare the room, my content, and my appearance. Instead, on the drive in, I saw flashing lights in my rearview mirror and ended up on the shoulder, heart pounding, wondering if I was going to be late for my crucial first meeting with the new staff.

In those minutes, a flood of emotions hit me. Frustration. Worry. Doubt. I feared this frustrating setback would define my first day. What would my staff think if I walked in late? Was this a bad sign for the year ahead?

Thankfully, the officer let me off with a warning, and I arrived on time. But I carried that rushed, unsettled feeling into the building. As I walked in, I realized I had a choice. I could let the chaos of the morning define my first day. I could choose to focus on my feelings of frustration, or I could take a deep breath and remember why I was there in the first place. Simon Sinek reminds us in his book, *Start With Why*, that when leaders put 'why' first, it changes culture, builds loyalty, and fuels motivation (Sinek, 2009). Our "'why' is deeply rooted in our purpose, and it's what drives passion and action. I could replay the rushed morning and stay in frustration, or return to the purpose of the day and prepare for a new year, lead my new team well, and choose joy.

At the Meet and Greet, I opened by sharing my morning experience. Instead of pretending it hadn't happened, I shared honestly. That small act of vulnerability broke the ice. People laughed with me, not at me, and it immediately created a sense of ease in the room. At that moment, trust began to take root. By admitting that things don't always go as planned, I showed my staff that effective leadership demands authenticity, a willingness to learn, and a deliberate choice in how we respond to setbacks. It is about being real, willing to learn, and choosing how to respond when things don't go as planned. I used this as a teachable moment to set expectations for what I knew would be a challenging year in teaching. I reminded my staff that the months ahead would bring challenges and unexpected turns. What would matter most was how we responded. I asked them to approach the year with grace, flexibility, vulnerability, and with the confidence that none of us had to do this alone. Our motto that year became, "We are stronger together." The choice I made to lead openly and honestly, by example, was a discipline I had built over the years, and it wasn't easy. When I was a new principal, I tried to hide my failures, weaknesses, and act like I had all of the answers. But this only sets the expectation that I want others to do the same.

When I first stepped into leadership, I had a big dream. I wanted to build a thriving school with a positive culture, foster lasting relationships, and lead a school where teachers loved teaching and students loved learning. I believed in collaboration, I believed in possibility, and that the heart of any school was found in the people who walked its halls. But as the days filled with discipline referrals, paperwork, and meetings that stretched late into the evening, my original vision started to seem unattainable. My sense of purpose felt like it was slipping away, and I was falling into survival mode.

This story isn't mine alone. Nearly every principal I've coached or worked alongside has faced this feeling. They began with a dream, filled with passion and purpose, but somewhere along the way, the sheer demands of the job left them frustrated, exhausted, and hopeless. That kind of burnout happens because purpose is not a one-time discovery you can set aside. It's something you must actively return to again and again, and continuous practice protects your deep conviction, ensuring you maintain the energy needed when the massive demands of leadership threaten to steal your focus. It is the anchor that holds when the demands of leadership start to pull you off course.

Before we move on, let's look at the definition of purpose. Purpose is defined as "the reason for which something is done or created or for which something exists" ("Oxford English Dictionary", n.d.). When the reason behind an action or program isn't clear, people will define that reason for themselves. For instance, a technology tool intended to enhance classroom instruction for students who finish early may inadvertently become the primary instructional method if teachers fail to grasp its purpose. Similarly, a Social and Emotional Learning (SEL) program purchased as a proactive, daily curriculum may instead become a reactionary measure to use only during student conflicts, missing its intended purpose. Establishing the reason something is done or why it exists is the lens that a principal uses to ensure that every action is intentional, every resource is well spent, and every initiative directly serves the school's purpose. This intentionality is the core of purpose-driven leadership, and it is the principal's fundamental responsibility to communicate this essential mission clearly. This clarity then becomes the foundation for the Four Pillars of leadership: People, Pedagogy, Processes, and Professional Growth.

Purpose-driven leadership is the discipline of tying every action and resource directly to the single result your school exists to achieve. It doesn't allow you to ignore difficult problems but demands that you confront them. Knowing your "why" instantly forces you to allocate your time and energy only toward vital results, not scattered effort. You stop reacting to every incoming trend and instead assess: "Is this action an investment in our mission?" Ultimately, you measure your success by impact, not activity and busyness.

This first chapter is all about discovering (or rediscovering) your why and learning to lead from it in a way that sustains you and inspires the people around you. You'll see that purpose goes beyond words. It guides your daily decisions and gives you strength when leadership becomes challenging.

Knowing Who You Are

For me, leadership starts with self-awareness and a deep conviction that what I do is making a difference. This belief has sustained me through challenging years and lonely periods when progress felt painfully slow and others resisted the changes I sought to implement. When you are clear about your purpose, you gain the confidence to keep moving toward your goal, even when achieving it takes longer than expected.

This sense of purpose changes everything. Knowing your "why" helps you decide what's actually important and protect time for it. Some days, everything feels urgent, and it's impossible to know what to do first or where to spend your energy. That's when your why becomes a filter. It helps you see what really needs your attention right now. You're creating the kind of school where both teachers and students can do their best work, where they feel supported, challenged, and valued. That's what makes the long hours and difficult moments worth it.

Within these foundational beliefs, each of us carries gifts, talents, and strengths that shape how we live. Assessments like The Six Types of Working Genius, the Enneagram, or the DISC can provide a common language for understanding strengths, preferred roles, and communication patterns. But these assessments can be helpful and only beneficial if we use their data to inform our decisions. The results should shape how teams are formed, who facilitates meetings, how communication is tailored, and how appreciation is shown. Without that follow-through, they're a one-and-done moment that is quickly forgotten.

My friend, Dr. Chris Owen, a professor and corporate business coach, believes everyone has an unfair advantage. It's the unique combination of gifts, talents, experiences, and perspectives that nobody else can replicate. It's not about being better than someone else. It's about being distinctly you. Your unfair advantage is what you bring to leadership that can't be taught in a course or copied from a manual. It's the natural strength you lean into, the perspective shaped by your story, the ability that feels effortless to you but powerful to others. Two principals might have the same leadership style on paper, but they bring completely different unfair advantages to their schools. It's the thing that sets you apart, the strength only you carry that your school desperately needs.

When you believe this about yourself, it frees you from trying to lead like someone else. You stop comparing yourself to the principal across town and start leading from who you actually are. But when you believe everyone on your team has an unfair advantage, it changes how you hire, how you delegate, and how you develop people. You stop trying to make everyone good at everything and start building a team where people's strengths actually complement each other. You put people in positions where their unique gifts can shine, rather than asking them to be good at everything.

One way I applied this in my leadership was by helping students recognize the same belief within themselves. On birthdays, I started using the intercom to announce: *"You were created on purpose and*

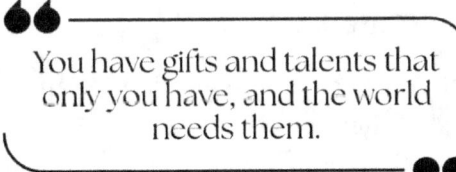

You have gifts and talents that only you have, and the world needs them.

for a purpose. You have gifts and talents that only you have, and the world needs them. We are so glad you are here to share those with us."

That message was simple, yet it gained immediate traction and rapidly became part of the school's culture. I had birthday cards made with that same message, and soon, students were memorizing it. They began repeating it to their teachers and to each other. We made shirts that said, "I was made on purpose and for a purpose," and sold them at school. They became one of the students' favorite shirts to wear. That phrase became more than words; it shaped how we saw ourselves and each other. Students began to believe they had a purpose, that their unique gifts mattered, and that being different was good. Teachers spoke over them. It reminded all of us that school is about more than grades and test scores. It's about helping each person discover their purpose.

That experience taught me something important. When you live from your purpose and lead from your unfair advantage, it spreads to others. Your clarity gives others clarity. Your conviction helps others believe in themselves. Every person in your building, staff, students, and parents, has a purpose and gifts and talents to bring. As the principal, part of your purpose is to help them see it, believe it, and live it.

When you know who you are and what your strengths are, you stop trying to do everything. You stop comparing yourself to other leaders and start appreciating the strengths you carry. You lead with clarity because you're not pretending to be someone else. You're building on the foundation of your purpose, doing the work only you can do.

Collective Purpose

If you've been in education for any amount of time, you've likely heard of the Ron Clark Academy. It's a school that people travel from across the country and the world to see. On the surface, it looks electric: students dancing in the halls, teachers teaching on tables, houses competing in chants and challenges. But the secret to their success isn't the show. It's the clarity in their mission, vision, and values.

At RCA, their mission and vision are thoroughly integrated into the culture, guiding the actions and decisions of every student, parent, and teacher, rather than merely displayed on their website. The result is a culture where every student feels seen, every teacher feels inspired, and every parent knows the school is about more than grades. It's about building citizens who will change the world. That's collective purpose: a shared mission, vision, and values that people can say, see, and practice together every day.

That's why the Ron Clark Academy is different than any other school. It's a living case study in the power of purpose. They succeed not because of charisma or energy, but because mission, vision, and values guide every decision, every conversation, and every behavior.

One Question

When I coach schools and principals who want help with culture, I always start with the same question: *What are your mission, vision, and core values?* Most of the time, I don't get a confident answer. Some leaders can quote a sentence that sounds similar to their mission statement, but aren't sure if it's the mission or the vision statement. Others recall a few aspirational words, such as "excellence" or "success," but struggle to explain what they mean in practice. I've had principals pull up their website or flip through the staff handbook to read the statements aloud because no one on the leadership team could recall them from memory. I once sat in a room where half the staff thought they were reciting the mission while the other half was quoting the vision; neither was right. These aren't careless leaders. They're committed, hard-working people. But without clarity on why their school exists, where it's headed, and how it's supposed to get there, the culture will reflect that confusion.

Even in schools that have done the work of writing thoughtful mission and vision statements, the practice often stops there, failing to translate into a daily, consistent guide for decision-making. They're using these to guide their decisions. They're not showing up in staff meetings, in classrooms, or in conversations with parents. Leaders may reference them once a year during the back-to-school in-service, but they're not woven into the daily life of the school. And when mission, vision, and values aren't applied and used, people default to survival mode, doing whatever they feel is best according to their own circumstances. Decisions are made based on urgency or pressure. Teachers are pulled in different directions. Students get mixed messages about behavior and expectations. Parents lose trust because they hear inconsistent messaging. Everyone is working hard, but not together.

On the other hand, when mission, vision, and values are defined, believed in, and lived out consistently, the impact profoundly influences the daily life of the school. A mission statement begins shaping decisions at the leadership level, new programs are adopted only if they advance the reason the school exists, and initiatives that don't fit are set aside, even if they're popular in another district. Vision provides direction for allocating resources, determining professional development, schedules, and budget lines, as it guides the school toward its intended goals rather than just meeting immediate needs. Core values are evident in the building's routines, the conduct of assemblies, the recognition of students for growth or kindness, and the approach to discipline conversations, which shift from punishment to restoration. Parents may not always agree with every outcome, but their trust begins to grow when they see the values consistently applied to decisions and conversations, regardless of who they speak with. This same consistent application is what allows students to develop a stronger sense of belonging when they experience core values in action. Teachers reinforce this essential culture daily by celebrating not only student achievement but also the choices and behaviors that actively reflect the school's vision.

When students feel a genuine sense of belonging in their school community, they are more likely to attend regularly, perform academically, and develop social-emotional stability (Balfanz, et al, 2024). That sense of connection isn't incidental—it arises when students see their school's mission and values reflected in daily interactions, expectations, and decisions. Research affirms that belonging grows when a school's vision is more than symbolic and is consistently visible in classrooms, routines, and community life. When students recognize that their contributions matter to the school's purpose, they move from participation to ownership. That ownership transforms not only engagement and learning outcomes but also the overall culture of the school community.

I've done this foundational work from the ground up in two very different settings, proving that purpose can transform any environment. In the first setting, I helped launch a brand new school. We had nothing but a blank page, and we spent hours debating words, clarifying what we wanted to stand for, how we would stand out in the community, and be different than every other school. It was fun, challenging, and exhausting, but it was absolutely worth the effort. When we opened our doors, we could feel the mission, vision, and values alive. Every decision—from the colors on the walls to the curriculum, schedules, programs, and electives—was determined by that clear mission and vision.

I've also stepped into a school that was more than forty years old, with long-established habits. Redefining the mission, vision, and values meant navigating history, honoring what came before, and carefully discovering what needed to change. That process was not quick or easy, but when we finished, the school truly began to come alive. Parents didn't just attend events; they volunteered, raised money, and championed the school's vision because they saw a purpose they wanted to be part of. Teachers felt the alignment, and they became excited about the future. I dedicated myself to building strong leadership teams, investing heavily in their development, and empowering them with the right tools and knowledge to succeed. That strategic investment paid off because these empowered leaders became absolutely essential in driving a profound cultural shift. I knew early on that a transformation this significant couldn't happen just through my effort alone. It required a collective, unified front, and my leadership teams stepped up, becoming the catalysts for positive change and fostering a shared sense of responsibility and growth across the school.

Research confirms what we experienced: Gallup's (2020) research shows that employees who understand and connect with their organization's values demonstrate significantly higher engagement and performance outcomes. The same is true for schools. When mission, vision, and values are clear, teachers, students, and parents don't just show up out of obligation; they serve joyfully and eagerly.

Getting there was not easy. Not everyone agreed at first. Some staff resisted, some wanted shortcuts, and many were tired of "one more initiative." We kept teaching the why and the how. We revisited the mission and vision in every setting, including staff meetings, PLCs (Professional Learning Communities), and professional development, and we tied practices and behaviors directly to our core values. We clarified what the words meant in daily routines, and we held each other accountable when decisions did not align. Over time, what felt like extra work became the way we worked. New initiatives stopped feeling like burdens because we were moving in the same direction. The hard conversations were worth it. The consistency paid off.

I often tell my leadership cohorts that turning a school is like turning a ship at sea. You do not spin the wheel and pivot in place. You set a heading, make minor corrections, and hold the helm through rough water. Culture moves a few degrees at a time with steady leadership, clear direction, and consistent follow-through. Some days, you will wonder if the hard conversations and collaboration are changing anything. Stay on course. The destination, a school alive with belonging, community, and shared purpose, is worth it.

That's why I always begin my coaching of new principals by helping them identify their school's mission, vision, and core values. They are the foundation that drives every action, behavior, conversation, and decision. Without a clear vision, schools often face recurring challenges. However, with a well-defined purpose, they achieve clarity, alignment, and a culture where individuals are not merely present for work but are deeply committed and invested.

> **"**
> Without a clear vision, schools often face recurring challenges. However, with a well-defined purpose, they achieve clarity, alignment, and a culture where individuals are not merely present for work but are deeply committed and invested. **"**

Distinctions Matter

Many leaders lack a comprehensive understanding of what mission, vision, and core values are, or how they differ. And that's not surprising. Very few of us were ever trained to write them, let alone to use them as tools for leading a school. I've worked with principals who use these words interchangeably, and others who admit they haven't looked at their statements since accreditation season. You're not failing if you don't have clarity here. But these distinctions matter. Each statement serves a different purpose, and together they form the foundation that keeps a school aligned. If you've never created them, you need to. If you already have them, they should be reevaluated every five years to ensure they remain current and truly reflect the dynamic needs of your school community. These three statements are the absolute foundation and starting point for everything we will explore in this book. They are the essential structure that supports the Four Pillars you will learn about in later chapters.

The mission statement defines your school's reason for existing. It is the core document that sets your school apart, clearly stating who you are and why you operate. A mission statement should be short and memorable, something every teacher, student, and parent can identify as unique to your school. Too often, mission statements are generic; *"We help students learn"* could describe any school in America. A true mission is distinct. One school I worked with rewrote its mission from a long, paragraph-length description to a single, bold statement: *"We exist to help children feel loved, respected, and encouraged to develop to their fullest potential."* That one sentence became the anchor for decisions. When leaders considered a new program, they asked: *Does this move us closer to our mission?* If the answer was no, the program didn't move forward. That clarity saved time, energy, and frustration while giving staff a renewed sense of direction.

The vision statement is your school's ultimate destination. It is future-oriented, painting a clear picture of what success will look like when the mission is fully lived out. A strong vision requires anticipation. It demands that leaders thoughtfully scan for challenges, trends, and shifts in educational policy, looking years ahead. This essential foresight helps staff and students see beyond the present moment and motivates them to continue moving forward in the same strategic direction. Without a guiding vision, schools quickly become complacent, settling for far less than their potential. With vision, schools look ahead and dream about what's possible. One school I coached created a vision statement where every student would graduate not only academically strong, but also confident, resilient, and prepared to impact their community positively. That statement shaped professional development, curriculum choices, and reframed conversations about student success. Teachers began to see themselves as builders of the future, not just instructors of content.

Core values are the shared principles that shape how a school community lives out its mission and moves toward its vision. They create clarity about what behavior, relationships, and decision-making should look like across classrooms and offices. Without that shared foundation, students and staff can receive mixed messages about expectations and priorities. At a school I helped coach, identifying values such as respect, responsibility, growth, and perseverance helped align daily practices with the school's mission. Teachers began recognizing students not only for academic achievement but for actions that embodied those values. Discipline conversations shifted from "Stop doing that" to "That's not who we are." Over time, those shared values turned aspiration into action, uniting staff, students, and families around a mission they could all clearly recognize and live out together.

If you haven't walked through this process before, here are the steps I use when coaching schools:

1. **Gather a diverse team.** Include school leaders, teachers, staff, parents, students, and community members. Broad involvement ensures multiple perspectives and authentic representation. This work is most effective when done collaboratively.

2. **Analyze your context.** Examine the school's demographics, community environment, family dynamics, culture, and student needs. Understanding your unique context grounds the statements in reality.

3. **Reflect on identity, purpose, and uniqueness.** Ask: Who are we? Why do we exist? What do we want for our students and families? How do we want to be recognized? What can we do that nobody else is doing? What sets us apart? This step helps clarify your school's distinct strengths and aspirations.

4. **Identify core values.** Articulate the guiding beliefs and behaviors that shape your school community and will support fulfilling your mission and vision. Ask questions like: What attitudes and actions do we want to see every day? What kind of environment supports learning and well-being? What principles inspire how we treat each other? Choose a manageable number (3-6) of concise, memorable values that describe how people should act to fulfill the school's mission and vision.

5. **Draft mission and vision statements.** Write the mission to clearly express what your school does now, who it serves, and the impact it seeks to have daily. The vision should articulate your school's long-term aspirations. What you hope to become and the difference you want to make in the future. Ask: What do we want our school to become? What is our ideal impact on students and the community in 5-10 years? The vision should motivate and guide long-term goals, expressing hope and ambition. Use simple, memorable language that everyone can understand and connect with. Avoid generic phrases by focusing on your school's unique purpose and ambitions. Be aspirational and inspiring.

6. **Gather feedback.** Share the drafts with staff, families, students, and community members to ensure they resonate and reflect lived experience.

7. **Refine and finalize.** Use the feedback to clarify and strengthen the statements. Prioritize authenticity and alignment between values, mission, and vision.

8. **Embed the statements into school life.** Consistently communicate and model them through policies, staff meetings, hiring, recognition, curriculum, and family engagement, so they guide culture and decisions daily.

This process makes mission, vision, and values meaningful, practical, and connected to your school community's identity and goals.

Once your school has clear mission, vision, and core value statements, the next critical step is to bring them alive. Here's how to do that effectively:

1. **Communicate consistently and clearly.** Share the statements regularly through meetings, newsletters, signage, announcements, and parent communications. Make sure the language is accessible and memorable.

2. **Teach their meaning.** Don't assume everyone understands what the statements really mean or look like in action. Use staff meetings, classroom discussions, and workshops to explore each statement:
    *   What does this mean for us as educators, students, and parents?
    *   How does it shape our daily decisions, interactions, and goals?

3. **Define mindsets and practices.** For each core value (and for mission and vision), clarify the attitudes and behaviors that bring them to life. For example:
    *   Respect: Listen actively, honor differences, and show kindness.
    *   Responsibility: Own your actions, meet commitments, and help others.
    *   Perseverance: Keep trying, learn from mistakes, stay focused.

4. **Model and reinforce.** Leaders and staff must embody the mission, vision, and values consistently. Recognize and celebrate when students and staff demonstrate these qualities. Use language that ties behavior back to the school's guiding statements.

5. **Integrate into routines and systems.** Embed the statements into hiring, evaluations, discipline approaches, student recognition, goal-setting, and professional development.

Make the mission, vision, and values a touchstone for all decisions.

6.   **Encourage reflection and ownership**. Invite staff, students, and families to share what the statements mean to them, where they see them practiced, and how they can contribute. This deepens connection and commitment.

Taking these steps turns statements from words on a wall into a living, guiding force that shapes your school culture, supports unified purpose, and drives better outcomes.

And if you already have a mission, vision, and core values, revisit them every five years. Schools change. Communities shift. Students face new challenges. What was clear ten years ago may no longer fit who you are now. It's part of the process of keeping the foundation strong.

The Purpose Lens

Let me tell you about a principal named Kelly. She'd taken the job knowing it would be hard. The school had been labeled failing, recruiting teachers was nearly impossible, and the community had lost confidence. But she loved the students, believed in the community, and wanted to build something that would make a real difference. She didn't expect to feel like she was drowning. Kelly was exhausted.

Everything screamed for her attention at once. Parents were blasting the school on social media. Some classrooms didn't have certified teachers. Students felt like they'd been dumped in a school nobody wanted to teach at or even be in. Teachers were on their own islands doing whatever they wanted. Some followed the curriculum. Others just showed movies to survive the day. Everyone kept asking Kelly for more programs, more technology, more resources to fix the mess. She couldn't get her footing. She didn't know where even to start.

Late at night, alone in her office, she began wondering if she was cut out for this job.

That's when she reached out for help.

When I heard her story, I understood why she felt paralyzed. The school had no mission statement, no vision, no core values. Nothing connected the staff to a shared purpose. They had every program and platform imaginable. Math enrichment, reading interventions, character curricula, multiple assessment systems, and technology tools piled on top of each other. But teachers cherry-picked what they felt like using and ignored the rest. Everything was supposedly important, which meant nothing actually mattered.

We didn't add another program. We went back to the fundamentals. Who are we? Why do we exist? Where are we trying to go? What do we value? As Kelly and her leadership team wrestled with those questions, something began to shift. A vision took shape. Clarity brought direction. Teachers stopped begging for more tools and started aligning them around a common objective. Kelly stopped second-guessing herself and started leading with confidence.

That's the power of what I call the purpose lens. Mission, vision, and values become the filter for every decision a principal makes. They bring focus when everything competes for attention, direction when choices pile up, and grounding for staff who need to know their work means something. Next, we'll look at the early signs that the foundation is cracking and the first steps to repair it.

When the Foundation Cracks

I'll never forget a season early in my leadership when I spent entire days reacting to everything and everyone that came to me. I would walk into the building every morning with a clear plan and great intentions. I wanted to send positive emails, call parents to celebrate their kids, work on our strategic plan, visit the cafeteria and playground to talk with students, and check in with my new teachers.

Those were the things I believed would make a real difference, the kind of leader I wanted to be.

But most mornings didn't go that way. Instead, I was met at the door by an upset parent demanding an unscheduled meeting. I got word that a teacher hadn't shown up, and there were no substitutes available to cover. Additionally, the internet was down, which meant frustrated teachers and an office scrambling to adjust. By 9:00 a.m., my purpose-driven plans for the day had been buried by whatever crisis felt urgent at that moment.

By the time I finally sat down in my office that evening, I realized I hadn't even looked at any of the things I had intended to do. I hadn't encouraged a single teacher. I hadn't checked in with students. I hadn't made any progress on our strategic plan. My dream of leading with purpose, of building culture, investing in people, and shaping vision, was put off for yet another day. This causes what I call cracks in the purpose foundation.

Here's what that season taught me: If you don't decide what gets your time, everything else will decide for you. The urgent will always take over. The urgent will always fill the space you don't protect. And when that happens repeatedly, it weakens the foundation you're trying to build.

> **If you don't decide what gets your time, everything else will decide for you.**

One of my turning points came when I looked at my calendar through a new lens. I pulled up a week's schedule and highlighted in green everything that directly reflected my purpose: time spent in classrooms, conversations with teachers, and vision-building work with my leadership team. Then I highlighted in red everything that was reactive or draining. By the end, my calendar looked like a stoplight stuck on red. Jim Collins reminds us in *Good to Great* that great organizations don't succeed by doing more; they succeed by the discipline to stay focused on their core purpose. That moment forced me to face reality: I was giving my best energy to the wrong things. My foundation was cracking, and I needed to take action. From that week on, I began making changes. I blocked out non-negotiable classroom visits. I scheduled one-on-one check-ins with teachers before the calendar filled up with other demands. Most importantly, I started filtering every request through a single question: Does this align with my purpose?

I saw this same challenge play out during a consulting visit with another school. Their principal was excited about launching a new technology initiative that was getting a lot of buzz in her district. When I asked how it aligned with their school's vision, she paused and stared at me for a moment. The truth was, it didn't. It would consume time, money, and energy without moving the school any closer to its goals. She took time to evaluate the initiative with her leadership team, and together they decided to pass on it. That decision freed her staff to invest their energy in strengthening relationships with parents and improving the learning environment for students. Implementing initiatives and programs that don't align with your mission or move you closer to your vision is what causes the foundation to crack. The foundation is your purpose, the mission, and the vision that should guide every decision you make.

When the foundation starts to crack, the best response is to slow down and take a clear look at what's causing the strain. Begin by paying attention to patterns, identifying areas where tensions are rising, and noticing when conversations that should be straightforward have become difficult. Review your calendar to see where your time is being spent compared to where it should be. Talk with your team and listen for what they're not saying as much as what they are. Review the routines and systems that once worked but now feel outdated or neglected. Those small signs often reveal the bigger issues, whether it's unclear expectations, a lack of clear and consistent communication, or too much on too few shoulders. Clarity comes from slowing down long enough to notice what's no longer serving the purpose, then rebuilding trust, restoring balance, and refocusing on the relationships that keep your school strong. Once you've identified where the cracks are forming, here's how you rebuild:

- **Recognize the cracks.** Notice when urgent tasks consume more of your time and essential work gets left undone. Pay attention when your calendar no longer reflects your values or when your team seems unclear about where you're headed. These are signs the foundation is weakening and acknowledging them is the first step toward repair.
- **Reclaim your purpose.** Once you understand what caused the cracks, return to your school's mission and vision. Bring your leadership team back to the why that should be driving every decision. Talk about it in meetings, reference it when evaluating new initiatives, and help your staff reconnect to the reason they chose education in the first place. A school that loses its purpose sees students suffer. Reclaiming it is how you rebuild the foundation.
- **Reset your rhythms.** Knowing your purpose isn't enough. You have to protect time for it. Block out classroom visits, one-on-one conversations with teachers, and vision work before your calendar fills with everything else. Build routines that keep your mission front and center. Aligning your daily rhythms with your school's purpose is what keeps the foundation strong.

When you bring your school back to its mission and vision, you create clarity for everyone. Your staff knows what they're working toward, your decisions make sense, and your team dares to lead from that shared purpose.

Helping Others Live Their Purpose

Purpose becomes unstoppable when it moves beyond the principal and into every person in the building. No school can thrive on the principal's purpose alone. When you're the only one carrying the mission, your staff will wait for direction instead of stepping into ownership. People can't live out their purpose if they don't first know they matter, they belong, and they bring something unique. The principal's job is to help them discover it.

One of the first things I noticed when I started this purpose-driven leadership journey was how many people on my staff were working in isolation. They couldn't see their own strengths, or if they did, they kept them to themselves. Teachers who had excellent classroom management were proud of what they'd accomplished, but instead of helping colleagues who struggled, they judged them for not measuring up. Support staff who built strong relationships with difficult parents felt superior rather than stepping in to share what they knew. The culture wasn't one of collaboration. It was one of comparison. Some had convinced themselves they didn't need to grow, that the old way of doing things was just fine. They weren't resistant because they were difficult. They were stuck because no one had helped them see that their gifts could build a great school together, not just prove they were better than everyone else. No one had helped them recognize their value beyond their job description.

They were stuck in their own classrooms, focused on their own success, unable to see the bigger purpose. Building a great school isn't about having a few strong classrooms. It's about creating a culture where everyone helps each other discover their gifts, where people learn and grow from one another. The principal has to create the conditions for that to happen, but they can't do it alone. Purpose has to move beyond the principal's office and into every hallway, classroom, and conversation. So how do you help people discover their purpose? You start by helping everyone see their value beyond their tasks.

Think about the staff. If teachers only hear about test scores, deadlines, data, assessments, and discipline, they begin to feel like cogs in a machine. Their work becomes transactional. They show up, deliver instruction, manage behavior, and go home exhausted because none of it feels personal or meaningful. That's when burnout sets in. When people are reminded of their inherent worth beyond performance, recognizing their strengths, voices, and unique gifts, it profoundly transforms their engagement and contribution to the team.

This is why I would start every year with a "My Favorites" questionnaire, a personality assessment, and a team-building activity that focused on appreciation. The point wasn't just fun activities. You matter as a person, not just as a position. Schools where this is ignored often become toxic environments in which to work. Schools that prioritize this approach create trust, foster a sense of humor, and retain staff.

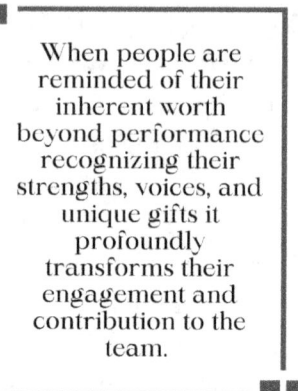

> When people are reminded of their inherent worth beyond performance recognizing their strengths, voices, and unique gifts it profoundly transforms their engagement and contribution to the team.

Students need to hear two things at once: you have a purpose, and here's how it fits our mission. Put the school's purpose in student language and invite students to discover their strengths. When students can say, "This is what I'm good at," and "This is where it helps what our school is becoming," they are more likely to participate, more likely to persist through difficult tasks, and more likely to look for ways to contribute beyond themselves.

Research from the Greater Good Science Center at UC Berkeley (2025) notes that students with a clear sense of purpose are more likely to report higher life satisfaction, more likely to persist through challenges, and more likely to seek out opportunities to contribute to their community. In school terms, that looks like steadier self-regulation, stronger focus during independent work, and quicker recovery when setbacks happen. When their strengths are identified and they can use them to further the school's mission, students are more likely to plan their work, monitor progress, ask for feedback, try a new strategy, and begin again rather than disengage.

Student recognition should reinforce the school's mission by celebrating when students use their strengths to support shared goals, whether through creativity, leadership, or organization. This recognition nurtures students' sense of purpose and motivation, leading to better collaboration, fewer disruptions, and steadier academic progress. Over time, these habit-forming behaviors driven by purpose and recognition contribute to greater achievement and a healthier school community.

One of the ways I invited student leaders to lean into their gifts and further our mission was a before-school Coffee Bean Club. We met every Friday, 30 minutes before school. I brought the coffee and hot chocolate. What surprised me was how many seventh and eighth-graders showed up that early. Maybe it was for the free coffee, but I like to think it was because they wanted to help solve problems and become better leaders. Using Jon Gordon and Damon West's (2019) book **The Coffee Bean,** we discussed the core idea of not letting difficulties in our environment change us, but instead changing the environment around us. We tied that idea to our school's mission each week and pointed it at real places on campus that needed a change. This morning meeting mattered because it gave students a sense of purpose and invited them to carry that purpose with them all day and change the environment around them. They were using their leadership skills to help me build the dream school and fulfill the vision.

As the group connected and we established trust, students brought to our meetings what they were seeing in hallways, at lunch, and during transitions, and we built small, practical responses that fit our values. I needed their eyes and ears; they needed to know their strengths had real authority inside our shared purpose. They only needed a leader who believed in them, cared about them, and took the time to invest in them.

Parents are another part of the foundation. If they're left on the sidelines, they'll hover, critique, or disengage. But when they are invited to participate in fulfilling our mission, even the most over-involved parent can become an ally. I remember one parent in particular was a constant presence in my office, worried about every detail of her child's life. It would have been easy to brush her off or try to hide when I saw her coming into the school. Instead, I decided to give her a responsibility. I recognized her gift of conversation and a desire to be valued and heard. She was a stay-at-home mom with time, and she was likable and personable. She had excellent ideas. She got out into the community and collected gift cards from businesses, items for our STEM program, and led our Teacher Appreciation Week. The result was the best celebration our school has ever had. When parents are invited to use their strengths in service of our purpose, they shift from bystanders to partners and become a source of strength.

The principal's role is to embody the mission and actively multiply that purpose across the entire organization. When purpose is communicated, understood, and shared from the front office to the classroom, from the teacher's lounge to the home, the culture becomes a supportive ecosystem where staff invest their energy, students thrive, and parents support the mission rather than hovering or critiquing. This active distribution of purpose secures the organization's stability over time and is the unmistakable mark of truly purpose-driven leadership.

> **The principal's role is to embody the mission and actively multiply that purpose across the entire organization.**

What Comes Next

A foundation exists in every school, shaping its culture and every decision, regardless of whether it has been clearly written down or is subtly practiced. Some schools operate out of survival, just trying to get through each day. Others function from pressure, chasing scores, pleasing parents, or jumping on every new initiative. Those foundations may keep things moving for a while, but they eventually crack. A school built on the wrong foundation may function, but it will never flourish.

Purpose is different. It is not one more thing to add to your plate; it is the thing that shapes how every other part of the work fits together. And it must be clear at every level of the school.

For principals, purpose means knowing your calling, your strengths, and the specific contribution only you can make to your school. It's the steadying force that keeps you from being swallowed up by the urgent and reminds you that leadership is about more than managing tasks; it's about shaping lives.

For teachers and staff, purpose means seeing themselves as more than employees filling roles. It's recognizing that their strengths and talents are needed, and that their presence and relationships matter just as much as their instruction. Staff who know their purpose show up differently. They stay invested even when the work is hard because they know they make a difference.

For students, purpose means more than academic achievement. It means understanding that they were created with unique gifts and talents that the world needs. When students are reminded that their kindness, leadership, growth, and effort are valued, school becomes more than a place to pass tests. It becomes a place where they discover who they are and how they can make a meaningful contribution.

And for parents, purpose means moving from outsiders or critics to true partners. Parents play a crucial role in strengthening the school's foundation. When their energy is channeled toward contribution instead of complaint, they become allies who build, not barriers to overcome.

Purpose forms the foundation we've been building throughout this chapter. From that foundation, four pillars emerge: People, Pedagogy, Processes, and Professional Growth. These pillars hold up everything a school does. In the next chapter, we'll explore the first pillar, People, and discover how purpose travels through the relationships that make a school thrive.

The Purpose Driven
Principal Framework

People

Purpose

Chapter 2

People: The Pillar of Relationships

I often opened our monthly staff meetings with a door prize. And to make it even more fun, when I said the words "door prize," everyone would clap and cheer. Fun was one of our core values. At our first all-staff meeting of the year, I set a coffee basket on the table and told the team that the first person who could stand and recite our mission from memory would win it. Several people tried, and came close, but no one could recite it exactly. I was glad for the engagement because it showed our culture had created a space where they felt safe enough to stand and try. My purpose was

> Fun was one of our core values.

not to test their memory but to assess our understanding. I learned that our mission, vision, and core values had not yet become part of our everyday language. People are the first pillar because they are the ones who determine whether the mission becomes a reality. The

> The leader's role is to build trust and continually bring everyone back to their core purpose.

leader's role is to build trust and continually bring everyone back to their core purpose.

The Relational Foundation

The ultimate success of any school is determined by the culture built among its people. A school can have the best curriculum, the newest technology, and the most detailed strategic plan, but if the people aren't connected, none of it works. Purpose doesn't live in documents or programs. It lives in relationships. The way a principal greets a struggling teacher in the hallway, the way a custodian speaks to a student having a rough morning, the way the office staff answers the phone when a frustrated parent calls.

> " A school can have the best curriculum, the newest technology, and the most detailed strategic plan, but if the people aren't connected, none of it works. "

People are the first pillar because human connection is the core necessity for all instruction, systems, and culture. You can't build strong instruction without strong teacher relationships. You can't create effective systems without staff who trust each other enough to speak up when something isn't working. You can't grow a positive school culture without students who feel safe and parents who feel valued. When relationships are strong, a school can weather almost anything.

This chapter is about building that strength. We'll look at how leaders create the conditions for trust to grow, how teams function when purpose drives them, how students thrive in a culture built on connection, and how parents shift from critics to partners. But first, we have to understand what makes relationships strong enough that people will take risks, speak up, collaborate, and stay committed when things get hard.

Trust: The Foundation of Strong Relationships

Trust is the invisible thread that connects people, stabilizes culture, and fuels collaboration. It's the invisible thread that connects people, stabilizes culture, and fuels collaboration. Research calls relational trust "the connective tissue that holds improving schools together," and the data backs it up. Schools with high trust see measurable gains in achievement, engagement, and well-being (Bryk & Schneider, 2002, p.44).

In 1914, Ernest Shackleton's ship Endurance was crushed by Antarctic ice, stranding 27 men in one of the harshest environments on earth. For nearly two years, they faced freezing temperatures, dwindling supplies, and impossible odds. Shackleton kept every single man alive. When they finally reached safety, his crew said they would sail with him anywhere. Why? Because Shackleton ate last. He gave up his gloves to men with frostbite. He never asked his crew to do anything he wouldn't do himself. He built trust through sacrifice and consistency, and that trust kept them alive (Shackleton).

While principals aren't navigating life-or-death conditions in Antarctica, the lesson remains the same. Schools face their own storms, and in those moments, trust is what holds people together. Trust is what keeps teachers from giving up, students from checking out, and parents from walking away. Trust is what allows schools to navigate difficult circumstances and come out stronger and more resilient.

> **"** Trust is what allows schools to navigate difficult circumstances and come out stronger and more resilient. **"**

John C. Maxwell says, "People don't care how much you know until they know how much you care." (*Developing the Leader Within You*) Trust develops when people consistently align their words and actions, communicate transparently, and demonstrate genuine respect and care. Students who feel they can trust at least one adult at school show greater motivation, confidence, and academic performance. The same is true for teachers. When educators trust each other, they share ideas, ask for help, and try new things without fear of judgment. Safety and openness replace isolation and competition.

Trust also strengthens relationships with families and the broader community. When you communicate clearly, follow through on what you say you'll do, and treat parents as partners instead of problems, they engage. They show up. They collaborate. Over time, this network of trust becomes self-reinforcing. Staff feel comfortable reporting struggles at an early stage. Students take risks in their learning. Families see the school as a dependable partner.

Trust isn't accidental. It doesn't happen just because you want it to or because you've stated it as a value. It's built deliberately through consistent actions over time.

Trust is earned through what you do, not what you say. To execute this, your leadership must be governed by these five non-negotiable principles:

- **Follow through on what you commit to.** If you tell a teacher you'll observe their classroom by Friday, be there by Friday. If you promise a student you'll check on their progress, check on it. If you tell parents you'll call them back, call them back. Every time you don't follow through, you teach people not to believe you.
- **Explain your decisions, especially the hard ones.** When you have to cut a program, change a schedule, or deny a request, tell people why. Don't hide behind "district policy" or "that's just how it is." When you can't share everything, say that and explain why. People can handle hard news. They can't handle being left in the dark.
- **Own your mistakes out loud.** When you mess up, say it. "I made the wrong call on that. Here's what I should have done." When staff see you admit fault without making excuses, they learn they can do the same. That's when real problems get solved before they explode.
- **Handle conflict in private, celebrate wins in public.** If a teacher needs feedback, close the door. If a staff member

does something excellent, tell the whole team. Protect dignity when you correct. Amplify value when you praise.

- **Be where people are.** Eat lunch in the cafeteria. Stand in the hallway during passing periods. Show up to the game, the concert, the play. Not because it's on your calendar, but because being present when it matters builds trust faster than any email or phone call ever will.

Trust takes time to build. It grows through small, consistent interactions over days, weeks, and years. When you're intentional about building it, trust becomes the most powerful thing your school has going for it

Building a Unified Team

In the Pixar film *Ratatouille*, a rat named Remy has an extraordinary gift for cooking. He partners with Linguini, a clumsy young man with no culinary training, in a struggling Paris restaurant that's on the verge of closing. On the surface, their partnership seems impossible. A rat secretly guides an inexperienced cook in a kitchen where perfection is everything. But they succeed, and what makes it work isn't just Remy's talent. It's the way he and Linguini build a unified team that trusts each other under pressure (Ratatouille).

Every person in that kitchen has a role, and they all understand it. The sauté chef handles the pans. The prep cook keeps ingredients ready. The expediter calls out orders and keeps the pace. Each person focuses on their specific task, but they also understand how their work connects to everyone else's. When orders flood in and the kitchen heats up, the team doesn't fall apart. They listen to each other. They communicate what they need. And when the toughest critic in Paris arrives to judge their work, the unified team delivers a flawless meal.

Schools operate the same way. Just like that kitchen, a unified team is built when everyone knows their role and trusts others to do theirs. The principal sets the vision and removes barriers. Teachers deliver instruction and build relationships with students. Support staff create the systems that keep the building running. Counselors address social and emotional needs. Each person contributes their part, and together they create something no one could accomplish alone.

Trust transforms how people work together. Teachers collaborate on curriculum instead of closing their doors. Support staff anticipate needs instead of waiting to be told. Leaders provide resources instead of micromanaging. Students experience adults working together toward a common purpose.

Schools thrive when people understand their roles, trust each other to contribute, and see how their work connects to something larger. That kind of team is built deliberately, one relationship and one interaction at a time.

With trust in place, unity grows when leaders know what motivates each person and show appreciation accordingly. A leader's ability to show genuine appreciation is a critical tool for building trust and keeping a team engaged.

For years, I thought I was doing this well. I handed out coffee gift cards, rolled themed "woot woot wagons" through the hallways with treats, put together birthday baskets, gave away door prizes at meetings, and left surprises in staff mailboxes. I publicly praised people and stuck encouraging post-it notes on their laptops. I meant every bit of it. But when I started using the assessments from *The 5 Languages of Appreciation in the Workplace* (2011) by Gary Chapman and Paul White, I discovered something that changed how I led. Only a few people on my staff actually felt valued by those gestures.

The book makes an important distinction: Recognition celebrates what someone does. Appreciation values who someone is. Recognition says, "Great job on that lesson." Appreciation says, "I see how you care about your students, and it makes

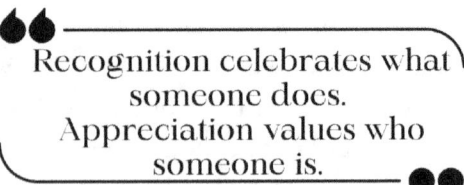

Recognition celebrates what someone does. Appreciation values who someone is.

this school better." Both matter, but appreciation goes deeper. It's personal. It's about the person, not just the performance.

When I looked at my staff's results, most of them ranked words of affirmation and acts of service as their primary appreciation languages. That meant my gift baskets and door prizes, while fun, weren't making most people feel truly seen. So, I changed my approach. I started looking for good things happening all around me. When I walked into a classroom, passed someone in the hallway, or sat beside them in a meeting, I looked for something specific to say out loud. Not generic praise, but genuine observation. "The way you redirected that student without embarrassing him? That's the kind of respect we talk about in our mission." "I saw how you stayed late to help that parent. Thank you."

For the staff who valued acts of service, I had to stretch my own capacity. I offered to help grade papers. I walked students to enrichment so a teacher could start planning early. I took a detention duty or ran an errand after school to grab supplies for a classroom party. Yes, it added to my workload. Yes, my capacity was limited. But here's what happened: It created a culture where people started doing the same for me. Staff began popping into my office on my busiest days and asking, "What can I take off your plate today?"

This is the power of intentional appreciation. When you learn how each person prefers to be valued and then consistently act on that knowledge, you show your team you don't just care about the work. You care about them as individuals. And when people feel genuinely appreciated, they invest more, collaborate better, and stay longer.

Appreciation and relationship-building can easily become the things you mean to do but never get to. They get added to the to-do list, moved to tomorrow, and before you know it, days turn into weeks. That's why this work has to go on your calendar. Your calendar doesn't lie; it shows what you actually value, not what you say you value. I printed out my staff list with their appreciation assessment results and committed to focusing on one or two people each week. I blocked time to be intentional about showing up the way they needed me to, whether that was words of affirmation in the hallway, helping with a task, or simply being present. What gets scheduled gets done. What gets done repeatedly becomes your culture. When staff see you consistently showing up for them, they know you mean it.

Every principal knows that their work is a collaborative effort, achieved through teams. While we'll explore the systems and processes that drive school improvement in a later chapter, those processes only work when the people implementing them trust each other and work well together. Teams are about relationships first, and meetings are where those relationships are built and strengthened.

A principal collaborates with various teams on campus, including the administrative team, a multi-tiered system of supports (MTSS) team, the leadership team, and a parent committee. The entire school itself is the ultimate team. But what makes a group of people a team? It's more than just a title or a meeting on the calendar. Great teams are built on purpose, trust, and shared accountability. They are a group of people committed to a common purpose, with clear goals and shared responsibility for achieving them. For school teams, meetings are the most powerful tool for building that shared purpose and holding the work together.

To establish strong, high-performing teams, every meeting must have a clear framework. These are the non-negotiables:

- **A Shared Purpose:** Before every meeting, a clear, one-sentence purpose and a simple agenda should be sent out. Directly tie the purpose back to the school's mission. A good start is a question like: "How will we ensure a smooth transition to our new reading curriculum?" rather than just "Reading Curriculum Meeting."

- **Clear Norms:** Establish a set of non-negotiable norms for every meeting and ensure they are consistently followed. This helps the work stay focused and keeps the team psychologically safe. Examples include: "Start and end on time," "Stay on topic," "One person speaks at a time," and "Disagree respectfully."

- **Defined Roles:** A facilitator, a timekeeper, and a note-taker can be assigned for each meeting. This ensures the meeting stays on track and that the work is captured. These roles can also be rotated to give everyone a chance to lead.
- **Actionable Outcomes:** A meeting should not end without clear, written next steps. Each step must have an owner and a deadline. This is where accountability lives. A meeting without next steps is just a conversation; a meeting with next steps is a work session.

End the meeting by scheduling the follow-up meeting. I call this **BAMFAM:** *Book A Meeting From A Meeting.* Scheduling a follow-up meeting at the end of every meeting transforms isolated conversations into ongoing progress, enhances accountability, improves collaboration, and nurtures trust within teams. It's a simple step that drives meaningful outcomes and efficient use of time.

Students First

Students are the reason a school exists. Period. Strong student relationships are the foundation because learning rests on trust. Research consistently shows that when students

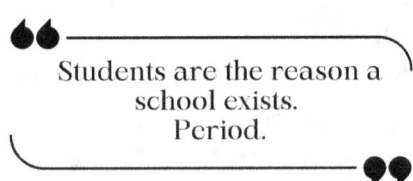

Students are the reason a school exists. Period.

experience close, steady relationships with teachers, engagement rises, motivation holds, attendance improves, and academic performance increases (Roorda et al., 2011). Students who feel supported develop self-efficacy, a sense of belonging, and resilience. They try longer, ask for help sooner, and recover faster after setbacks. The opposite is also true: distant or inconsistent relationships fuel disengagement, behavior problems, and academic struggle. Stronger social skills and fewer behavioral issues in later years are consistently predicted by positive teacher relationships established early on (Hamre & Pianta, 2001). These connections have a lasting impact.

A principal's role is to make those relationships predictable and visible across the day. That starts with presence. Be at the doors in the morning. Walk the halls when students move. Spend time in classrooms and the cafeteria to learn their names and stories. Follow up when a student has a hard morning and help them restart. Presence tells students, "You are seen, and you matter here."

Principals also build student relationships indirectly by equipping the adults who see students most. Coach staff in establishing simple, repeatable practices that deepen student trust, such as greeting at the door, using clear routines, correcting in private, and giving specific praise that acknowledges their effort. Create schoolwide structures that make connection routine. This includes a check-in plan, so every student has an adult who notices them by name each week, a short, dignified repair process after conflict, and a welcome routine for new students so belonging starts on day one. Put the mission into student language and use it in everyday interactions so expectations feel human and shared.

All structures, goals, and routines should exist to help students thrive, but without strong relationships, every one of those efforts will fail. The principal is the lead relationship builder. By being visible to students, knowing them by name, and setting simple systems that prioritize connection and trust, the leader creates the conditions where students feel safe, invest effort, truly learn and grow.

Building a culture of trust with students required me to step out of the traditional principal role and choose deliberate acts that earned their confidence and showed them that learning could be fun. It looked like putting on hair nets and aprons with my assistant principal and working the lunch line every day for two weeks when we were short-staffed. It looked like taking a pie to the face after a reading goal, moving my desk to the roof for a fundraiser, and climbing into the dunk tank at the fall carnival. It looked like laughing with students in the hallway and then kneeling beside a desk to help a child start over after a hard morning. None of this was random. It was intentional. I wanted students to see a principal who was approachable, trustworthy, and relatable. I made time for it. I chose to be outside during drop-off and dismissal. I arranged my schedule to prioritize these moments.

Fun breaks down the walls that authority naturally creates. Danny Bauer asks a question every principal should answer: if learning isn't fun, what are we even doing here? When students see you laugh, take risks, and celebrate with them, they learn school isn't just about compliance and consequences. They realize that learning itself can be enjoyable. Fun creates curiosity. Curiosity creates lifelong learners. That kind of culture can't be built through rules and procedures alone.

Those moments broke down the distance that can exist between my office and the classrooms. When students watched me roll up my sleeves in the cafeteria line, or saw me celebrate a school win by getting soaked or slimed, they learned something about authority that a thousand rules could not teach. They discovered that adults could be both firm and kind. They knew that adults would keep their word. They learned that adults were willing to look a little silly for the sake of establishing a positive culture that honors our core values.

When principals model this work instead of simply expecting it from others, the entire school culture changes. Older students step into leadership. New students find their place. This is how the mission meets students in ordinary moments, and why relationships must always come first.

Partnering with Families

A relational culture can scale with students, but it will not last unless families are part of it. Research states that when families are actively engaged, students attend more regularly, behave better, earn stronger grades, and build healthier social skills. They develop self-belief and resilience, and they are more likely to pursue college after graduation. Classrooms with strong family engagement see gains for all students, not only those with involved parents. Authentic partnerships also build trust. Families feel valued and understood, and teachers gain insight that helps them teach well.

Too often, the first principal-parent conversation happens during a problem. Choose a different pattern. Make the first contact a positive one. A thirty-second call about a kind choice, a quick note home, or a positive office referral sets a new tone. Add simple welcome routines that repeat for every new family. Hold a brief meet-and-greet, host a coffee chat, and share a short "how we do school" overview that explains how to contact the teacher and office, what to use for messages and grades, and who to call for which issues. Clarity protects the partnership.

At one school, we built this into a required Partners in Education Night. The name said the purpose: partnership. We served coffee and pie, then set two goals. First, we explained our mission and how it shaped daily practice. Second, we made roles and routines clear so families knew how to help their children succeed. After the assembly, teachers walked parents to classrooms and showed them the systems they would use: how to reach the teacher, what to expect in weekly updates, what homework looks like, and how behavior is addressed. The evening was not a lecture. It was a start to a working relationship. In the weeks that followed, parents echoed the same language at home that students heard at school, and small problems were solved early because people knew whom to call and what to expect.

The power of strong school-family partnerships is undeniable. When schools and families work together, students gain comprehensive support, leading to improved attendance, increased effort, and a positive shift in the school environment. While a principal cannot achieve this alone, their leadership is crucial in establishing this pattern. By being proactive, clear, and involving parents in meaningful ways, principals can forge partnerships that provide students with a level of advancement no single program can match.

Won't You Be My Neighbor?

A thriving school cannot exist in isolation. Its mission is only as strong as its connection to the surrounding community, including local businesses, neighborhoods, and even families without students in the building. A school is not just a building. It is a promise. It promises parents that their children will be safe, cared for, and prepared for the future. It promises students that their potential matters and someone will invest in helping them discover it. It promises the community that the next generation will be equipped to lead, serve, and contribute. A school is the single most powerful institution a community possesses, a living testament to its belief in the future.

Community partnerships don't happen by accident. They happen when principals step out of the building and start conversations. I made it a practice to approach local business owners and community leaders, ask to meet with the manager or owner, introduce myself, and share information about our school. I recognized them as great service providers to our staff and families, and if nothing else, I wanted to thank them and acknowledge the role they played in our community. But I also offered them a partnership opportunity. I invited them to see our school. When they arrived, I had students greet them at the door, introduce themselves, and show the respect and character we were building as part of our mission. I walked them through the spaces we were developing, explained our vision, and then sat down over lunch to just genuinely talk.

The results were tangible. Our local grocery store, where many of our families shopped, provided a monthly donation for teacher snacks and food for our professional learning community meetings. Another store gave us a substantial financial contribution to launch our STEM program. Our local bank served at our school every August for their community service project, cleaning up our playground. An art facility donated supplies to start our art program. A local children's gymnastics company stored extra bars, mats, and equipment so we could offer weekly gymnastics for students. A community art program started hip hop dance and a drama club after school. Summer programs included chess lessons from a businessman who loved the game, frisbee golf from a local enthusiast, and tennis from a nearby club.

These partnerships created momentum. When the community invests, it sends a message to everyone that something meaningful is happening here. It tells staff, "I'm glad I work at a school the community believes in." It tells students, "I'm glad I go to a school that people want to support." And it tells families, "This is a place worth being part of." When the community is aware of needs and sees a school worth investing in, they partner. But it starts with the principal stepping out, making the ask, and building the relationship.

Navigating Difficult Conversations

Difficult conversations are not a matter of if they will occur, but when. You can't have genuine relationships without conflict. The question is not whether conflict will happen, but whether it will be healthy or destructive.

Healthy conflict moves a team forward. It surfaces problems early, clarifies misunderstandings, and strengthens trust when handled well. Unhealthy conflict festers in silence, damages relationships, and erodes culture. The difference is not in whether people disagree, but in how leaders navigate those moments.

A leader's ability to navigate difficult conversations is a powerful opportunity to build and deepen trust. When done well, these conversations become affirmations of a school's commitment to its people and its mission. The purpose is not to win an argument or assert authority, but to preserve and strengthen the relationship. As Jon Gordon (2024) points out in his book, *Difficult Conversations Don't Have to Be Difficult*, our goal should be to approach these discussions with a positive mindset, focusing not on the problem, but on the positive outcome we're working toward.

Preparation is key before having any difficult conversation. Before a meeting, take a moment to reset your intent and purpose. Write down the simple facts, list the single core value at risk, and set a one-sentence goal for the meeting. Choose a private room, set a specific time limit, and keep your phone face down and silenced. Open the conversation with calm words that demonstrate a shared purpose: "Let's start by talking about what happened, then discuss what a positive outcome looks like, and finally, plan how we can get there." Then, listen without interrupting, summarize what you've heard, and identify areas of agreement. The agreement can be written before anyone leaves the room, and a follow-up date can be set. Document what happened so no one has to retell the story. That rhythm maintains dignity and moves the work forward, no matter the context.

With parents, the overarching goal is to get on the same team, because when a school and a home work together, the student benefits. When a parent first comes to you upset, your primary job is to listen without reacting. They may just need to vent, and in that moment, your calm presence is the most powerful tool you have. A simple, empathetic response, such as "I hear how upsetting this is, and I want to help," can de-escalate the situation. Rather than relying on opinions, bring concrete work samples or behavioral notes to the meeting to support your claims. This deliberate approach, grounded in purpose, lowers the emotional temperature and keeps the conversation focused on a solution that is best for the student.

With teachers, a difficult conversation is a powerful opportunity for coaching and growth. A principal's most important role is to support the people on their team, encouraging them to become the best teachers they can be. The work of Patters, Grenny, McMillan, and Switzler (2018) in *Crucial Conversations* provides a robust framework: when stakes are high and emotions are strong, we must create a "shared pool of meaning." This is how you make it safe for everyone to contribute their perspective without fear of judgment. The goal is to move past a power struggle and into a genuine dialogue. In all cases, a principal's role is to create and protect this psychological safety. By establishing a safe space, you invite everyone to move toward a unified solution. The focus must remain on the work, not the person. Ground the conversation in a specific incident and avoid broad, emotional language. Use clear examples and offer one specific support, and set a date to see the change. When progress is made, it should be announced and celebrated.

This process focuses on establishing a consistent, predictable approach that fosters trust and progress, rather than on having all the solutions. The ultimate aim is to cultivate teamwork, whether among students, teachers, or parents.

The Pillar That Holds

The People Pillar holds the most vital component of your school: relationships. Relationships. Without strong relationships built on trust, no curriculum succeeds, no system functions smoothly, and no mission comes to life. A school's purpose is where everything begins. The People Pillar is where that purpose finds its life. A mission statement, while a powerful story on its own, truly comes to life and becomes a reality through the strong relationships cultivated with staff, students, parents, and the wider community. This pillar, built on an unwavering foundation of trust, shifts a school's culture from a collection of individual rooms and agendas into a unified place with a shared heartbeat. The result is a culture of belonging.

Belonging is what you feel when you walk into a school where relationships are strong. You see it in the teacher who greets every student by name at the door. You hear it in the

> " A mission statement, while a powerful story on its own, truly comes to life and becomes a reality through the strong relationships cultivated with staff, students, parents, and the wider community. "

laughter that fills the hallway between classes. You notice it when the custodian stops to help a kindergartner tie their shoe, when the office staff knows which parent needs a translator before they even ask, when students hold the door for each other without being told. Belonging shows up in the way new families are welcomed on their first day and the way veteran staff still feel excited to come to work. It's present when a struggling student knows exactly which adult to find when they need help, and when that adult drops everything to listen.

In a culture of belonging, every person feels valued and safe. Staff aren't afraid to admit when they need support. Students take risks in their learning because they trust the adults around them. Parents partner with the school instead of working against it. The community invests because they see something worth supporting.

The work of building a culture where people truly belong is never accidental. It is the principal's most essential legacy. When relationships built on trust form the heartbeat of a school, every action, every conversation, and every decision carries purpose. This unity sustains all learning and growth. Staff, students, and families who feel seen and valued bring your mission to life. The People Pillar transforms a collection of individuals into a connected, thriving community. That lasting sense of belonging is the truest mark of leadership.

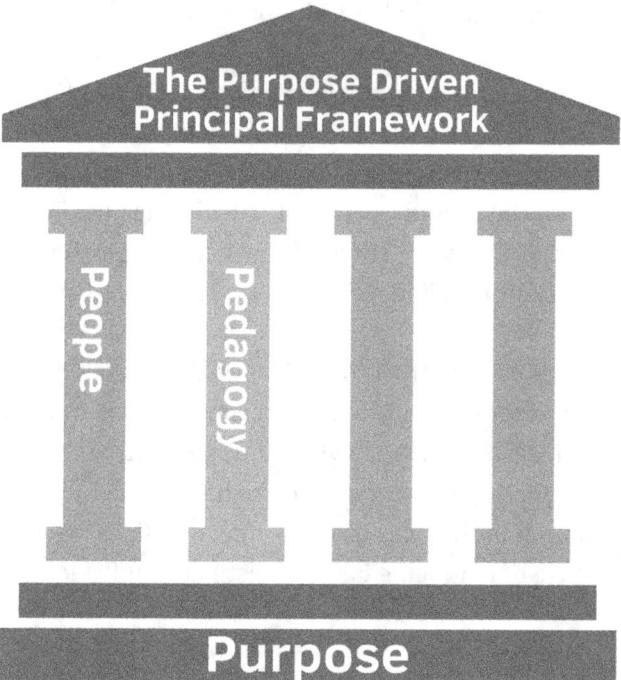

CHAPTER 3

Pedagogy: The Pillar of Learning

The Missed Lesson

I could have heard a pin drop. I walked into the classroom, and every student was sitting in perfect rows, quietly filling in blanks on a worksheet. The teacher sat behind her desk, reading from the text, her lesson plans neatly aligned to the standards. At first glance, it appeared to be a well-managed classroom. The pacing was tight. The content followed the curriculum.

I could have walked away thinking, *What an orderly classroom. What great classroom management. What careful alignment to the standards.* But one question pressed in: were these students actually learning?

It made me wonder if we had ever been clear enough as a staff about what great teaching and great learning should look like in our school. Had we tied it back to our mission, vision, and values, or was each teacher left to interpret it on their own? And just as importantly, had we agreed on what our priorities would be when it came to classroom learning? With this clarity, teaching transforms into a shared pursuit of purpose, rather than a collection of individual preferences.

Good teaching delivers the curriculum and manages the classroom well. It demonstrates preparation and skill. But great teaching goes deeper. It connects what students learn to why it matters and how they'll use it beyond the classroom. Great teaching ensures that students not only receive information but also understand, apply, and grow from it. It creates an environment of trust, so students feel safe taking risks. It motivates them to engage, not just comply.

Research supports this distinction. Studies from the Sutton Trust (Coe et al., 2014) found that the strongest predictors of effective teaching are deep content knowledge, high-quality instruction, clear explanations, thoughtful questioning, and meaningful practice. John Hattie's *Visible Learning* (2008), highlights teacher clarity, feedback, and collective efficacy as among the most powerful drivers of student achievement. Great teaching is measured not by how quiet or orderly a room appears, but by its impact: student growth, engagement, and mastery.

> Great teaching is measured not by how quiet or orderly a room appears, but by its impact: student growth, engagement, and mastery.

This chapter is about how a principal leads the work of defining what powerful teaching and authentic learning mean for their school. That work has to be shaped by the mission, vision, values, and goals of the community you serve. What works in a large suburban high school in California may not apply to a small rural high school in Nebraska. Purpose-driven pedagogy requires clarifying what great learning looks like for your students in relation to your mission and then guiding your teachers in implementing it.

Pedagogy is the art and science of teaching: the methods, practices, and strategies educators use to help students learn. In a purpose-driven school, pedagogy becomes the how and why behind every learning experience. It's the daily choices teachers make about instruction, assessment, engagement, and relationships. When pedagogy is purpose-driven, those choices are intentional, grounded in the school's mission, and focused on student growth. This pillar holds the instructional core of a school, ensuring that teaching produces learning aligned with who we say we are.

Keeping Learning at the Center of the Mission

Not long ago, I attended a PLC team meeting where the conversation centered on the content that had been taught, the number of lessons remaining in the unit, and whether the pacing guide would allow them to complete the unit before the test. Everything sounded efficient and on track. However, as I listened, I realized a critical question was missing: Where are students in their learning process? Are they mastering the skills we expect them to? What evidence is present in the data?

That moment solidified my belief that mission lives or dies in the classroom. Since a school's mission is a promise statement. Pedagogy is the action that either keeps or breaks that promise. Every day, the methods teachers use, the questions they ask, and the ways students are engaged either align with that promise or they don't. If the mission says, "cultivate critical thinkers," but instruction rests on memorization and recall, the promise is being broken. Mission and vision aren't just statements on a wall; they are reflected in daily teaching.

This is why I lean on the four guiding questions of Professional Learning Communities (DuFour & DuFour, 2019):

- What do we want students to learn?
- How will we know if they learned it?
- How will we respond when they don't?
- How will we respond when they already know it?

Each question depends on data. Evidence from student work, exit tickets, and short common assessments turns reflection into action. When setting a goal, we also specify the data to review and the evidence to look for in determining its effectiveness.

These questions may seem simple on the surface, but they are rigorous in practice. They shift the focus from teaching to learning, from coverage to clarity. They help us see honestly where students are and whether they're meeting the goals we've set, using data and evidence, not impressions.

As principals, our work is to keep these questions at the center of every instructional conversation. In team meetings, we check whether the focus is coverage or learning. We build structures to review data, make time to examine student work, and protect grade-level reflection so teachers can answer these questions with honesty and depth.

Purpose-driven pedagogy isn't measured by how many standards are "covered" or how tidy the pacing calendar looks. It's measured by whether students are learning in ways that reflect who we say we are as a school.

The Principal's Role as a Learning Leader

When I first became a principal, I assumed my role in instruction was to ensure teachers had the necessary resources and then step aside so they could do their work. Over time, I realized that wasn't enough. If student learning is at the heart of our mission, then I had to lead it, not by controlling classrooms, but by shaping a culture where growth was expected and supported by everyone.

Being a learning leader doesn't mean being the best teacher in the building or micromanaging every lesson. It means guiding the culture so that student learning is always the focus. As one recent synthesis of research put it, "Principals are most effective when they are instructional leaders who guide their schools toward student-centered practices, supporting teachers in responding to the diverse needs of their learners" (Learning Forward & Wallace Foundation, 2021).

Leading the learning culture requires being the one who champions student growth, models humility, and creates the conditions where teachers can take risks. When principals lead this way, instruction moves from individual isolation to collective ownership, making student achievement the shared focus of the entire school.

Defining What Great Teaching and Learning Look Like in Your School

Effective instruction and meaningful student learning depend on clear, shared expectations among educators. Each teacher brings individual strengths, but excellence is achieved when there is a consistent understanding of what quality teaching looks like. This common vision shapes daily practice, supports collaboration, and ensures all students experience purposeful learning. Defining what effective instruction and authentic learning require creates the foundation for student growth and success.

But here's the challenge: what does excellent teaching actually look like in your school? Not in a research study. Not in another district. In your building, with your mission, serving your students.

This is where the principal's leadership matters most. You cannot assume teachers will naturally align their instruction with the school's mission unless you guide that work. You have to bring the staff together and ask: What does excellent teaching look like here? What does authentic learning look like for our students? How do we know when we see it?

These conversations require clarity and specificity. If your mission says you develop critical thinkers, what does critical thinking look like in a kindergarten classroom versus a fifth-grade classroom? If your vision includes student voice and choice, what does that sound like during a math lesson? If your values include respect and perseverance, how do those show up in daily instruction?

The principal's role is to facilitate these conversations, not dictate the answers. Bring grade-level teams together. Show video clips of instruction that align with your mission. Examine student work samples. Ask: Does this reflect our mission? Does this align with what we say matters?

This work takes time and requires revisiting the conversation regularly, especially as new staff join the team. When a school has a shared understanding, instruction improves across the building. Feedback becomes specific and actionable. New teachers know what's expected from day one. Students experience consistency across classrooms.

Excellent teaching in your school should reflect your mission. The principal's job is to lead the work of defining it clearly, so every teacher understands what constitutes effective teaching for the benefit of their students.

Building a Culture of Evidence and Growth

A culture of evidence and growth is one where every instructional decision is intentionally rooted in student data. This focus is essential because clear evidence shows teams exactly where students are and what is genuinely needed for individual progress. This allows leaders to make informed, student-centered decisions while keeping the overall mission in sight.

Student growth requires intentional planning and decision-making guided by relevant and actionable evidence. A principal doesn't need to be a statistician, but they do need to help teams see which data diagnoses learning gaps and points toward specific solutions. When teachers are buried in numbers that don't connect to student growth, they become disengaged, unsure of where to invest their time, and lose their instructional focus. Principals can help teachers frame data as evidence of learning rather than compliance, shifting the culture away from checking a box for the principal and toward making informed decisions for every student. Pedagogy without this guidance leaves instructional decisions based on intuition, opinion, or convenience rather than proven need. We'll explore the systems and processes for managing data in the next chapter, but understanding why evidence matters for instruction comes first.

It is crucial to use a range of evidence, including Formative Assessments (such as exit tickets and observations), Summative Assessments (such as exams and final projects), Diagnostic Assessments (such as baseline tests), Performance-Based Assessments (such as presentations and portfolios), and Benchmark Assessments (such as periodic monitoring). The value of this evidence is unlocked only when leaders structure the data so teachers can easily access the findings and translate them directly into their next lesson plan. The ultimate goal of a culture of evidence is achieved when the principal creates a safe environment that allows teachers to openly discuss what the data reveals, even when the results are uncomfortable or discouraging. When this system is in place, assessment becomes purposeful and contributes to a sense of collective efficacy. Teachers stop relying on differing opinions on what a student needs to succeed and start responding with precision, ensuring instruction is tailored to where students are and interventions target true gaps.

Systems That Support Learning Together

Every student deserves a team of adults working together to help them succeed. Kurtis and Lorna Hewson (2022) remind us of this truth in their work on Collaborative Response. This happens by building systems that bring teachers together with a clear focus on student learning.

Too often, only students who are failing receive the support of a team. Students on the

> **Too often, only students who are failing receive the support of a team.**

cusp, those in the middle who aren't struggling enough to raise alarms but aren't thriving either, often slip through without intervention. When schools don't ensure every student has a team working on their behalf, those students eventually become the ones who need intensive support. Shared responsibility for every student must become part of how the school operates. This requires the principal to ensure that collaboration is built into the school's structure and focused on what all students need.

This next section describes several systems that have worked in my schools and in many others. Your school may use different structures or adapt these to fit your context. The goal is not to copy what works elsewhere but to build collaborative systems that serve your students and align with your mission.

Professional Learning Communities provide the foundation for collaborative work. Regular team meetings focused on the four questions from earlier in this chapter: what students should learn, how we'll know they understood it, and how we'll respond either way. These meetings keep the work grounded in student learning. PLCs shift the focus from what was taught to what students learned.

WIN Time—What I Need (McConnell, 2019) offers one practical example of design in action. Using grades, missing assignments, assessments, and teacher input, students can be grouped into three-week rotations that align with their individual needs. Placement and movement are data-driven. Evidence from grades, assessments, missing work, and teacher input guides every decision, so support is intentional rather than based on guesswork. Some students receive targeted support in math or reading, while others focus on strengthening their study skills. Those ready for a challenge pursue enrichment activities, such as STEM projects, digital learning, intramural sports, or structured study halls. While every school's model will differ, the principle remains: design must ensure that every student has a clear plan and a meaningful next step.

Another powerful design tool is the **Model Classroom** approach described by Ashlee Boothe. A model classroom is not about showcasing one "perfect" teacher; it is about creating a shared picture of what effective teaching looks like in that school's context. Visits are anchored in student data and classroom evidence, prompting the question: What did students produce? Who was ready to move on? How did the teacher know? Teachers visit, observe, and reflect on the practices that align with the school's mission and vision. Together, they design strategies for consistency across classrooms, ensuring that students experience a coherent vision of learning, regardless of which class they are in (Boothe, 2022).

Through these collaborative approaches, whether PLCs, WIN Time, or Model Classrooms, pedagogy becomes a shared responsibility focused on student learning. Teams work together to ensure every student receives what they need. The principal's role is to create the time, establish the structures, and protect the focus so teams can do this work well.

> " Teams work together to ensure every student receives what they need. "

The specific systems you choose for your school will depend on your context, your students, and your mission. What matters is that you build collaborative approaches that ensure every student has a team working on their behalf and that pedagogy serves all learners with intention and purpose.

Connecting Practice to Purpose

The hardest part of connecting practice to purpose is implementation. Every practice in a school sounds good in isolation. Professional Learning Communities improve collaboration. WIN Time supports struggling students. Data teams strengthen instruction. Professional development builds teacher capacity. Model classrooms create a shared understanding of excellent teaching. But when everything is a priority, nothing is a priority, and it becomes difficult to know where to focus. The gap between knowing and doing comes from poor implementation support. Implementation research in educational settings shows that translating new ideas into action is a prolonged journey requiring more than good intentions (Forman et al., 2019). Most school improvement efforts fail because goals are unclear or too numerous. Professional development happens once and then disappears. Teachers return to classrooms without ongoing coaching. Data sits in spreadsheets instead of driving decisions. Resources don't align with what teachers are being asked to do. And perhaps most damaging, schools abandon practices before they have time to take root.

Successful implementation depends on clear communication, resource allocation, fostering a culture receptive to change, and addressing barriers like resistance and workload (Alsubaie, 2024). The connection from information to action requires deliberate implementation, ongoing support, and patience. What will we try first? What will we stop doing to make room? Which teachers need coaching to implement this well? What evidence will tell us if it's working? How will we provide sustained professional learning instead of one-time training? How long will we commit before we evaluate whether this practice is producing the outcomes we expect?

Purpose provides the filter for making decisions quickly. When you know what matters most, you can act on incomplete information because you're moving toward something clear. Implementation succeeds when purpose guides which practices matter, leadership provides sustained support, and the school commits to giving those practices time to create real change.

The principal's role is to bridge the gap between research and practice by setting clear goals, aligning resources, providing ongoing coaching, celebrating early wins, and protecting time for practices to take root (Adelman & Taylor, 2019; RTI International, 2023). Purpose guides which practices to implement. Strong leadership ensures those practices move from idea to action and stay long enough to transform learning.

Persistence Over Perfection

Principals and teachers often confuse persistence with perfection. We think if we just plan better, train more thoroughly, or explain more clearly, the practice will work flawlessly from day one. When it doesn't, we assume something is wrong with the practice, the people, or the plan.

Striving for perfection leads to frustration, burnout, and paralysis. Persistence fosters steady progress through setbacks and allows deeper mastery over time. Cultivating problem-solving combined with patience rather than chasing perfection shifts the mindset of both principals and teachers. Accepting struggles as a natural and integral part of implementation builds resilience and encourages creative problem-solving when challenges arise. The goal is progress, not perfection.

Meaningful change takes time. Research shows that seeing measurable positive impact from new

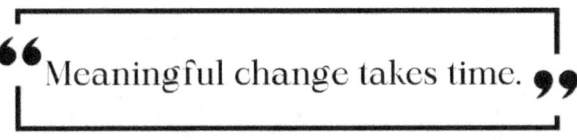
"Meaningful change takes time. "

initiatives often takes three to five years, especially when changes involve shifts in teaching practices and school culture (IES, 2025). Yet principals and teachers expect immediate results. When data doesn't improve in the first semester, the practice gets blamed. Teachers feel overwhelmed by one more thing, and without adequate support and collaboration, they give up. The initiative dies before it ever had a chance to work.

New practices rarely work smoothly at first. Teachers stumble through early attempts. Data often dips before it rises. Students resist changes to routine. Parents question what's different. This discomfort is normal, but schools treat it like failure. Principals move to the next initiative before the first one takes root. Teachers retreat to what they know because trying something new feels too risky.

Persistence requires a culture shift. The principal can't be the only one making tweaks and adjustments. Encouraging teachers to shift from problem-presenters to collaborative problem-solvers requires principals to model this mindset, clarify roles, and facilitate decision-making that balances input with ultimate leadership accountability (District Administration, 2024). When teachers co-create solutions instead of waiting for the principal to fix everything, persistence becomes shared responsibility.

When leaders and teachers focus on results and persist until those results are realized, the work of the school becomes aligned and effective. Students acquire the skills intended, teachers accurately recognize effective instruction, and data reflect meaningful progress. This focus creates a coherent system where effort is aligned with clear goals. Persistence drives this coherence because real change takes time and comes through steady progress, not flawless execution. The commitment to keep moving forward despite obstacles ensures that school goals are measurable outcomes that improve learning every day.

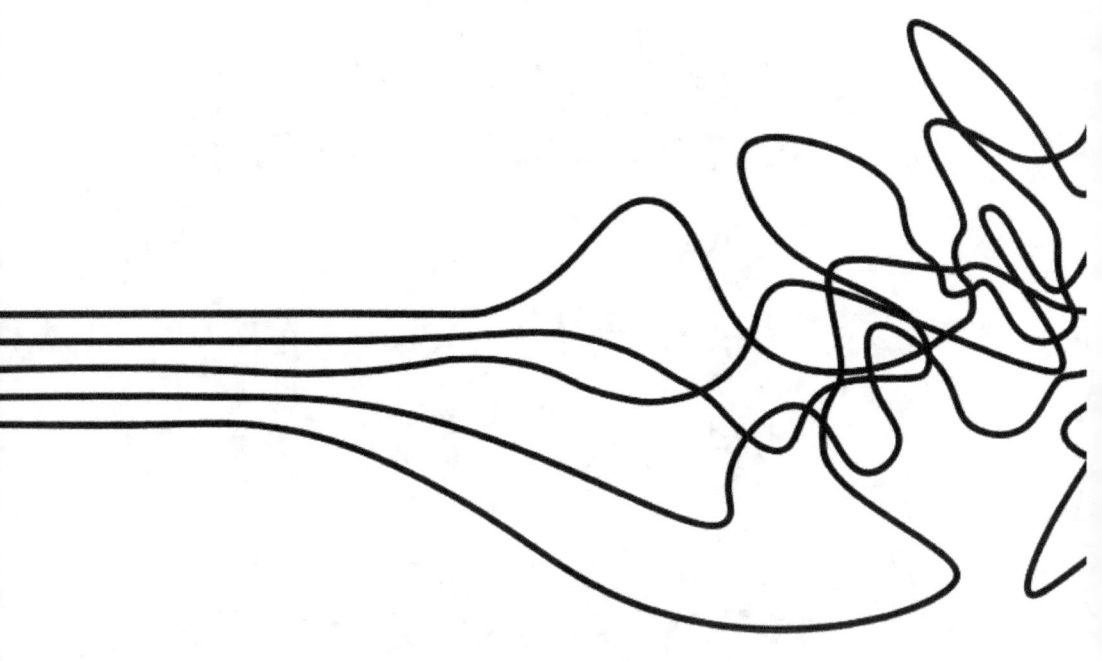

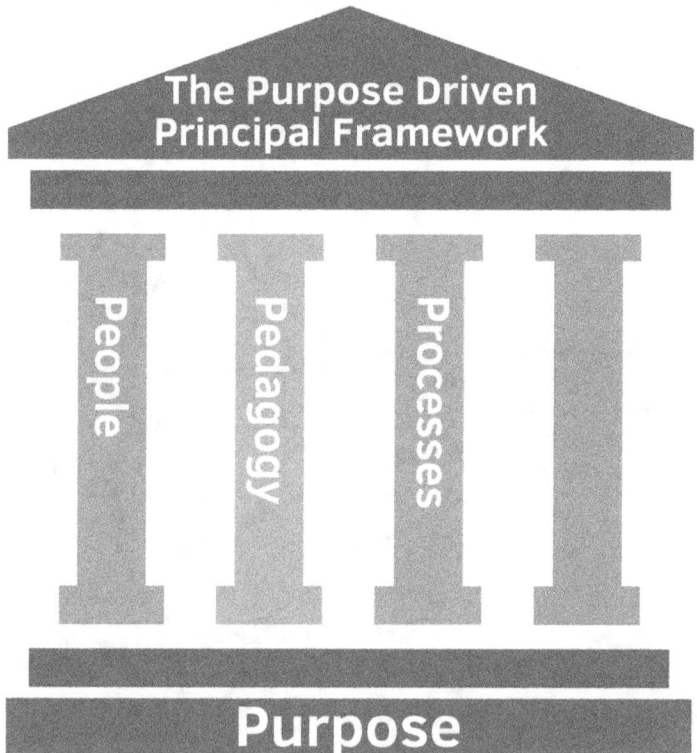

CHAPTER 4

Processes: The Pillar of Systems

When I first moved from faculty to leadership, I worked harder than I had ever worked in my life. Each day felt like a marathon with no finish line in sight. I was pulled in ten different directions as I supported teachers, helped new staff, planned events, and managed the steady flow of issues that landed on my desk. By spring, I thought I had finally found a rhythm.

When the next school year began, I expected all that hard work to make things easier. Instead, it felt like I was starting over. We had organized a major fundraiser the year before, but because we had kept so few notes, planning it again meant recreating the whole thing from scratch. We had migrated to a new Student Information System but had not created training guides or videos, which meant onboarding new staff required hours with one-on-one explanations. Assistants and registrars had developed solutions, but since nothing was documented, their work disappeared the moment they moved on. Even something as routine as submitting field trip requests became confusing because no one could remember the process.

> That is when I realized the problem was not the people. The problem was the lack of systems in place.

That is when I realized the problem was not the people. The problem was the lack of systems in place. I had built year one on memory and long hours instead of on processes that could be repeated. And as soon as people shifted roles, or as soon as I forgot, I was back at the beginning.

Many schools struggle with processes and procedures that are either unclear, outdated, or were never created in the first place. The result is wasted time, constant interruptions, and leaders forced to reinvent the wheel year after year. When systems are weak or missing, everything defaults to the principal because no one else knows who's responsible or what steps to follow. I learned the hard way that unclear systems keep principals stuck reacting to problems instead of leading strategically. When expectations are clear, work is shared effectively through delegation, and every person knows their role and the steps to do the work well, the job becomes more sustainable for everyone.

Clarity and Confidence

Clear processes and procedures do more than save time. They bring order to daily work and give people confidence in how to carry it out. The purpose is clarity and repeatability. Good processes and procedures help people know what is expected, why it matters, and how to do it well. Systems make the work function reliably instead of depending on individual people to remember everything.

Casey Watts, author of **The Craft of Clarity** (2025), writes, "The work of clarity is not for the faint of heart, but it is for those who believe in something bigger than themselves. It's for leaders who want to leave teams better than they found them. It's for those willing to reflect, monitor, and adjust when things go off course, as they inevitably will" (p. 171).

Clarity is not only something you have. It's something you create. And it's a leadership skill that's not often developed. It determines whether your team runs in circles or moves in one direction. Principals who create clarity through strong processes give their teams the ability to move forward with confidence. Without clarity, even the most capable people waste energy trying to figure out what to do and how to do it.

Schools rely on three interconnected structures to create this clarity: policies, processes, and systems. While these terms are often used interchangeably, they serve distinct purposes. Understanding the difference helps leaders build the proper structure for the right need.

Policies set direction. They act like guardrails, outlining what is allowed and what is not, so the school stays aligned and consistent. Good policies prevent confusion and ensure that decisions align with the school's mission. They keep everyone moving in the same direction, even when opinions differ or pressure builds to cut corners.

Processes provide the step-by-step path to reach a goal or outcome for an activity. A process spells out what needs to happen, in what order, and what the desired outcome looks like. Clear processes remove guesswork and help people feel confident in carrying out their role. Well-defined processes ensure work is repeatable, reducing reliance on individual memory or experience.

Systems are much larger and more impactful than a checklist or procedure. A system is a collection of related processes, combined with the people responsible for the work and the tools that support them. A strong system answers who does what, when it happens, which resources are used, and where the guide can be found.

When processes are unclear, people are left to guess. When systems are weak, the work relies on memory or the knowledge of a single person. People do not fail. Systems fail.

Get It Out of Your Head

Together, policies, processes, and systems provide schools with the structure they need to function effectively without leaning on the principal for every answer. The purpose of all three is clarity, repeatability, and sustainability. Strong systems shift the load from people to processes, ensuring that work continuity is maintained even when someone leaves. They simplify jobs, reduce stress, and create space for leaders to focus on what matters most.

I still remember the knot in my stomach when a member of my admin team told me she'd be going on a 12-week maternity leave. Of course, I was thrilled for her, but underneath the joy was a very real anxiety I didn't say out loud: How will we manage without her? What if we drop the ball on everything she handles that no one else is aware of? That fear was a wake-up call. To prepare, I asked her to document every responsibility step by step, including examples and notes. I told her, "I need you to get what's in your brain onto paper for me." The binder she created was so helpful that it sparked an idea.

If one binder could keep essential responsibilities from slipping through the cracks, what would happen if everyone created one? That became the start of our Brain Binders. Each person developed a monthly checklist outlining tasks that needed to be completed every month and every year, with precise details on who would perform them, when they were due, and how they should be executed. Each Brain Binder included examples, notes, and resources, allowing the work to be repeated with confidence. Staff brought their "brains" to every meeting, and over time, we built a collection that held the steps for every position in the school.

Once the Brain Binder System was in place, the work no longer depended on memory or a single person. It was housed in a system accessible to the entire team. With those steps written down, our work became easy to share, sustain, and repeat. That freed me, as the principal, to focus on supporting the teachers, strengthening instruction, connecting with students and parents, and shaping the school's culture.

Strong systems do more than keep the daily operations clear and repeatable. They also give us a way to think about data. Schools collect information daily, ranging from attendance and behavior to SEL, grades, and skill mastery. However, without processes, procedures, and systems, these numbers rarely lead to improved teaching or learning. Data only becomes meaningful when purpose and processes give it direction, enabling informed decisions and effective action.

Data-Informed, People-Driven

Collecting data does not change student learning. Change occurs when schools utilize data through clear processes, procedures, and systems that connect numbers to action. As Jessica Lane writes in Clarity, Connection, Momentum (2023), schools should be data-informed and people-driven because numbers alone do nothing without people interpreting and applying them with purpose.

This shift in language matters. A data-driven culture reduces students and teachers to numbers. It pressures leaders to chase percentages instead of supporting people. Principals must lead their schools away from that mindset. Being data-informed means we value evidence, but we let it guide rather than dictate decisions. Being people-driven means students and teachers stay at the center of every conversation.

When a principal leads with this perspective, data becomes a tool for growth instead of a weapon for compliance. Attendance reports are not just red flags. They serve as reminders to check in with families. Behavior data is not just about discipline. It is a window into relationships and culture. Academic data is not just a score. It is an insight into how we can support students in mastering the next skill.

Processes explain the work of data. They set the rhythm for what is collected, when it is gathered, and who reviews it. Procedures add consistency, ensuring that data is recorded, stored, and discussed in the same way every time. Systems bring it all together with roles, timing, and tools so the cycle continues year after year.

The purpose of these structures is not compliance. It is impact. Data should always lead to the next step. If attendance dips, the school responds and measures whether it improves. If behavior incidents rise, the team introduces SEL supports and watches for patterns to change.

If mastery lags in a skill, instruction is adjusted, and growth is monitored.

Schools continually cycle through a rhythm of using data to understand, respond, and measure. Data becomes more than information, integrating into the culture of learning.

Essential Processes That Keep Schools Moving

Essential processes turn everyday tasks into reliable systems that reduce stress and confusion. Clear communication channels ensure parents, staff, and students receive consistent information. Structured onboarding helps new teachers settle in and thrive. Disciplined meetings focus on actionable outcomes instead of consuming time without producing decisions. Yearly rhythms for tasks like end-of-year procedures prevent June chaos and enable smooth transitions into the following year. These processes shift reliance from individual memory to documented, accessible systems, allowing leaders to focus on the mission instead of reacting to whatever crisis demands attention.

George Bernard Shaw is widely quoted as saying, "The single biggest problem in communication is the illusion that it has taken place." Every principal has lived this reality. You send an email assuming everyone reads it. You announce something at a meeting, thinking it's clear. You tell a teacher the plan and believe they understood. Then

> The single biggest problem in communication is the illusion that it has taken place.

you discover people are left more confused or have more questions than before you communicated.

This happens because leaders assume a message has been understood when it hasn't. Communication systems prevent this illusion by closing the gap between what leaders think they've communicated and what people actually understand. Leaders must work deliberately by increasing communication frequency, choosing the proper channels, and encouraging feedback. It takes clear purpose, active listening, and follow-up to ensure communication is not just sent, but actually received and understood. Being intentional about this prevents misunderstandings, builds trust, and aligns teams around common goals.

Communication is an ongoing narrative, not a series of isolated events. A single announcement at a staff meeting will not be remembered. People need to hear it multiple times, in various formats, before it becomes real. Face-to-face conversations create clarity. Written messages create

Communication is an ongoing narrative, not isolated events.

reference points. Group discussions surface misunderstandings before they become problems. When communication occurs through varied channels and is consistent, shared meaning replaces assumptions.

Effective communication builds connection by giving people what they actually need. Families don't need daily updates. They need a single reliable source for crucial information. Staff don't need more meetings. They need structured time for planning and collaboration where they can express their views and be heard. Students don't need constant reminders. They need adults (teachers, parents, and administrators) who communicate effectively with one another, so they don't have to manage the learning gaps themselves.

Strong communication systems also create safety. When students know they can share concerns without punishment, they speak up about problems adults can't see. When staff feel heard rather than managed, they bring solutions rather than complaints. When parents receive transparency rather than silence, they become partners rather than critics.

Build communication systems around clear roles and repeatable processes. Who sends the newsletter and when? Who responds to parent emails and how quickly? Who checks in with new staff and on what schedule? Answer these questions once, document the process, and the system runs without constant oversight.

Communication either connects people to the mission or leaves them guessing. The difference is whether you've built a system that makes communication predictable, accessible, and understood. Three other processes are just as essential: onboarding new staff, running effective meetings, and establishing yearly rhythms. Each requires a clear structure and consistent execution.

New staff arrive with energy and expectation, and the way we welcome them sets the tone for their future. A straightforward onboarding process provides them with the tools, training, and cultural cues they need to thrive from day one. Pair this immediate support with 30, 60, and 90-day check-ins to provide structured feedback and support. These touchpoints prevent small challenges from escalating into reasons to leave and demonstrate to staff that growth and clarity are integral to the culture.

End-of-year checklists are another vital piece. Without them, the month of June becomes a chaotic scramble. With them in place, tasks are closed out smoothly, equipment and records are secured, and the following year begins with confidence instead of confusion.

And, of course, there's the challenge of meetings. Every leader has experienced sessions that consume valuable time without producing clear results. As organizational expert Patrick Lencioni observes in **Death by Meeting** (2004), the core issue isn't the frequency of meetings; it's the absence of intentionality in them. To transform meetings from obligations into strategic assets, you must treat them as an operational process:

1. Define the Purpose: Every meeting must begin with a single, clear objective stated on the agenda.
2. Focus on Action: The discussion should be strictly focused on reaching a decision and assigning clear action items.
3. Ensure Follow-up: Meetings must end with a clear accountability plan that outlines specific responsibilities and deadlines for each task.

When you master this process, meetings become essential tools that align your staff to the mission and drive schoolwork forward.

Strong systems don't appear overnight. They're built by identifying where confusion, frustration, or inefficiency shows up repeatedly. I learned to treat every knock on my door, every question about how to do something, every phone call or email asking what something meant as a gap in a system, in clarity, or in communication that needed to be addressed. These moments showed me where systems were missing or weak.

What's predictable is preventable. When the same question gets asked multiple times, when staff reinvent the wheel every year, when

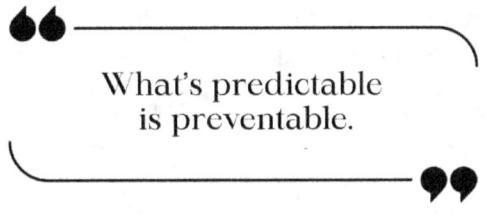

What's predictable is preventable.

tasks fall through the cracks despite good intentions, those are signals that a system needs attention. Take note of these patterns. Teachers who say, "I never know how to..." are pointing to a missing process. Office staff who say, "Every year we scramble to..." are showing you a weak yearly rhythm. Parents who say, "I didn't realize..." are revealing a communication gap.

Once you identify a gap, decide whether you need to strengthen an existing system, tweak one that's almost working, or create something new. Strengthening means clarifying roles or documenting steps that currently live only in someone's head. Tweaking means adjusting a process that works but could be more efficient or inclusive. Creating means building a system from scratch where none exists.

Prioritize based on what's costing you the most time. Start with which gaps cause the most stress, waste the most time. You can't fix everything at once, but you can tackle the systems that make the biggest difference. Use your Brain Binder approach or whatever documentation method works for your team. The key is getting the process out of people's heads and into a repeatable system.

Systems aren't built to control people. They're built to serve people and the mission. When you identify gaps and strengthen weak systems, you create the structure that allows people to do their best work without burning out. This stability becomes the strategic foundation that builds your team's capacity, giving everyone the time and focus needed to engage in high-impact leadership and instructional work.

Communication, onboarding, meetings, and yearly rhythms create the operational structure that keeps schools running. But systems alone don't lighten the principal's load. That requires intentional decisions about what work stays on the principal's plate and what gets shared with the team. It requires the courage to delegate, the wisdom to protect time, and the discipline to say no to good things that don't serve the mission. Lightening the load happens through systems that share the weight and leaders who know they can't carry it all alone.

Lean In

One summer, just after college, a group of friends and I went whitewater rafting in West Virginia. When we arrived, the guides informed us that they were short-staffed and offered us a choice: we could split up and ride with other groups that had guides, or we could stay together in a raft of our own. We hadn't driven six hours to end up with strangers, so we stayed in the same boat, even though it meant going without a guide. At twenty-two, confidence and courage came easily, but we didn't yet understand that those things aren't the same as being prepared and experienced.

Before we launched, one of the guides leaned over and gave us a warning. *"If the rapids slam you into a rock, don't lean away. That's what your body will want to do, but it will flip you out. Lean toward the rock and put your weight there."*

For the first stretch, the river was manageable. We paddled and found a rhythm that gave us a sense of control. But about an hour in, the rapids picked up and grew rougher. We were struggling a bit but still managing until the raft slammed into a boulder, and precisely what the guide had warned us about began to unfold. Our first reaction was to push away from the rock, which was the one thing the guide had warned us not to do. The raft started to climb the face of the rock. We tried to scramble across and throw our weight the other way, but the angle was too steep. Within seconds, the boat slipped and flipped us into the freezing water.

What I remember most is the second before we flipped. The guide had told us to lean toward the rock, but every one of us leaned back. We made the wrong move, and the raft slid up the boulder and tossed us into the river. We weren't short on courage or determination, but we hadn't set ourselves up for success. We chose to go without a guide, convinced we could manage on our own. That decision put us in a difficult position because when the river turned rough, we lacked the experience and support to make the right move. We ended up scattered and had to finish the trip in other boats, which was the very option we'd been given at the start. Leaders fall into the same mindset trap when they convince themselves they can manage everything on their own. Principals throw themselves into the work with long hours and big hopes, believing they can carry it all until the school they dream of finally takes shape. And for a while, it works. However, when leaders fail to delegate to their team, lean on their experience, and follow wise coaches, the weight eventually becomes too heavy to carry. That is how burnout begins.

Lightening the Load

Delegation is a central theme in every leadership conversation because principals know its value firsthand. However, delegation alone doesn't ease the demands leaders face. The real shift begins with recognizing which tasks never needed to be on a principal's plate and making conscious choices about what to say yes to. Each day brings countless requests, and the difference between sustainable leadership and burnout lies in intentionally handing off, delaying, or removing some of those demands.

Not everything can be delegated or removed. State deadlines arrive. Parents expect answers. Student needs come up without warning. What can change is the response. Leaders can set boundaries for what remains on the principal's plate and what is shared. They can determine which evening events require the principal's involvement and which can be handled by assistant principals, deans, or teacher leaders. They can protect non-negotiables, such as taking lunch without the laptop, going for a short walk outside when the weather allows, and setting aside a block of time each week with no meetings.

> " The gap begins to close when the discipline required today feels lighter than the overwhelming feeling that often accompanies a yes to everything. "

Most principals already know these ideas. The gap is not one of knowledge, but of action. Moving from awareness to action requires daily discipline and commitment. The gap begins to close when the discipline required today feels lighter than the overwhelming feeling that often accompanies a yes to everything.

While there's no single solution to lighten the load principals carry, this section will explore some of the most impactful approaches. One of those solutions is delegation. Done well, delegation is a big part of the answer. Principals need a straightforward way to organize their work and build systems that enable others to take ownership of it.

In my new principal coaching cohorts, I guide principals through a process that helps them categorize their responsibilities into four areas: what must remain with the principal, what can be shared, what can be delegated to others, and what can be eliminated.

For anything being delegated, the process includes clear steps. First, set expectations by being explicit about what the task is, why it matters, and what success looks like. Second, build in checkpoints at critical moments to provide support and ensure alignment without micromanaging. Third, debrief afterward to discuss what worked, what didn't, and what needs to shift next time. Finally, document the process so it can be replicated or refined moving forward.

One principal who went through this categorization identified twenty-seven primary responsibilities on her plate, and by the end of the process, half had been reassigned. This exercise works because delegation needs structure. This approach develops capacity in others while genuinely freeing up the principal's time and energy.

Granting genuine ownership is arguably the most challenging transition when delegating. This involves allowing individuals to tackle tasks in their unique ways, even if they diverge from the principal's preferred methods. It also necessitates providing space for mistakes, as failure frequently serves as a crucial element in the journey of growth. Effective delegation is about fostering empowerment and cultivating leaders capable of advancing the work.

When the right work is shared, structure becomes the part that keeps the rest of the job from collapsing back onto the principal. Effective, consistent systems create space for people to stay at the center of the work. The following practices are simple examples that have made a measurable difference for the principals I coach.

- **Meeting guardrails.** Cluster meetings on two or three set days each week. Leave at least two days open for classrooms, planning, and follow-up. The goal isn't fewer meetings, but wiser placement that protects focus.

- **Email windows.** Check and respond at two scheduled times each day. Use a short auto reply noting those times and who to contact for urgent issues, so the inbox doesn't rule the day.

- **Event coverage map.** Build a yearlong list of evening events. Mark which events truly need the principal and which can rotate among assistant principals, deans, or teacher leaders. Sharing the load makes leadership more sustainable for everyone.

- **Stop-doing review.** Once a month, list the routines and reports that fill the week. Decide what to keep, what to simplify, and what to eliminate. Every hour reclaimed is one returned to purpose.

- **Parent hours**. Offer two weekly blocks for parent conversations. Predictable windows reduce interruptions, allowing for calmer, more thoughtful communication.

- **Walkthrough blocks.** Schedule classroom visits in focused blocks and leave one clear, timely note for each teacher. Feedback improves when attention is undivided and purpose stays centered on growth.

These strategies may not be revolutionary; however, they are practical and profoundly effective. Each deliberate move, from strategic scheduling to intentional delegation, works to remove hidden weight and alleviate the often-overwhelming burden from a principal's shoulders, allowing them to lead with greater clarity, purpose, and impact.

Small pauses help keep our purpose in view when the day starts to run the leader instead of the other way around. A few quiet minutes to reflect, walk a hallway, or listen without an agenda can reset one's perspective and bring the work back into focus.

Take a few minutes to answer the questions below before proceeding. Reflection isn't a luxury in leadership; it's an essential practice that maintains strategic focus.

Reset Prompts
- Where do I create intentional space in my week to reflect?
- What parts of my job remind me of why I lead?
- Which tasks or interactions energize me, and which leave me depleted?

- Where can I pause briefly each day to regain focus?
- Who provides steady support and perspective when leadership pressures become overwhelming?

Processes and procedures may not be as exciting as a new curriculum or leadership training, but they represent the reliable infrastructure that supports every successful school. Systems protect your team's focus and capacity. Delegation shares the load and develops leaders. Time-protection strategies create the calm and consistency needed for instruction and learning to thrive. When processes are purposeful, repeatable, and sustainable, and when work is shared wisely, they become an indispensable pillar of success. The stability achieved through sound process design and wise delegation enables personal growth and development. The vital importance of that growth for the leader is the subject of our next pillar: Professional Growth.

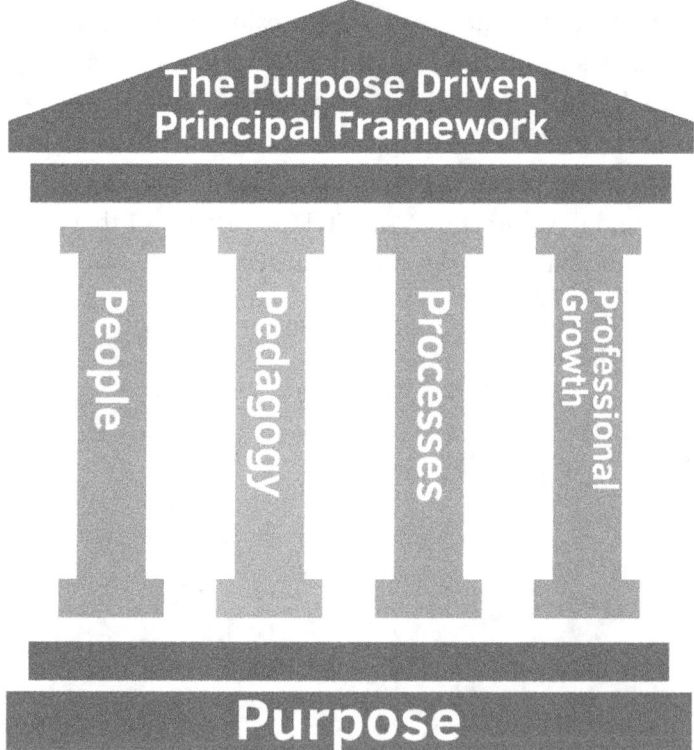

CHAPTER 5

Professional Growth: The Pillar of Progress

Professional growth is the pillar that equips principals to rise above the immediate pressures of the job. It is what allows leaders to move beyond survival mode and continue leading with clarity and conviction. Growth expands perspective, sharpens judgment, and cultivates the skills necessary to navigate a school through complexity. Before you can lead others well, you must first lead yourself.

Leading yourself well begins with understanding your strengths and leading from what you do best. It requires acknowledging the weight that comes with leadership and finding sustainable rhythms that prevent burnout. It demands reflection that turns experience into wisdom and builds the self-awareness needed to handle stress and make better decisions. It depends on connection with peers, mentors, and coaches who provide perspective, accountability, and shared learning. And it requires ongoing investment in your physical, mental, emotional, and spiritual well-being. Together, these practices create the capacity to sustain leadership without burning out, model growth for your staff, and ensure the school thrives because you are thriving.

Growth happens when information and action come together to develop habits. Reading a book or attending a workshop provides knowledge, but knowledge alone doesn't change leadership. Growth occurs when you take what you've learned and put it into practice repeatedly until it becomes part of how you lead. As James Clear writes in Atomic Habits (2018), "If you can get 1 % better each day for one year, you'll end up thirty-seven times better by the time you're done"(p.15). Small, consistent improvements compound over time. That's how principals build the capacity to handle the demands of the role without burning out.

> **"** If you can get 1 % better each day for one year, you'll end up thirty-seven times better by the time you're done. **"**

Burnout in leadership rarely stems from a lack of passion. It arises when the demands of the role outpace the preparation and support needed to meet them. Growth bridges that gap. It creates space for reflection, offers new tools, and reconnects leaders with their purpose. When growth is absent, the role becomes a cycle of reaction and exhaustion. When principals invest in their own development, it acts as a buffer and source of renewal that empowers them to sustain their leadership.

The evidence is clear. Each year, a significant number of principals leave their schools, which unsettles teachers, families, and students. One of the main reasons is that the demands of the job outpace the preparation and support they receive. That's where professional growth makes the difference. Leaders who continue to learn are more likely to remain in their positions because they feel equipped, supported, and confident. And when they stay, the people they lead are more likely to stay with them.

Most importantly, professional growth shapes culture. When staff see a principal who is still learning, still curious, and still willing to improve, it sends a powerful message: growth is not just for students. It is the way forward for the entire community. Growth boosts morale, fosters trust, and makes the work worthwhile.

The Fire Hydrant

In one of my group coaching cohorts, I asked the principals how they were doing. One sighed and said, "It feels like drinking from a fire hose." Another quickly chimed in: "I'm not drinking from a fire hose— I'm drinking from a fire hydrant." We all laughed at her analogy, but the truth behind it wasn't funny at all. That image captured the crushing pressure she felt every single day. The constant flow of demands, discipline issues, staff needs, parent complaints, and district requirements was more than she could handle.

That feeling of being overwhelmed is not sustainable. No leader can keep absorbing that level of pressure without a release valve. And yet, this is precisely where many principals find themselves, stepping into leadership with limited preparation and support. Many schools do provide some sort of mentor or coach for new principals. Still, several of these principals end up in my cohorts and have stated that once-a-month conversations with a district-assigned mentor don't teach you how to manage the flood of responsibility.

Every principal will face the hydrant at some point. The difference is that growth equips you to withstand the pressure, not be consumed by it.

Professional growth is the work of becoming the kind of leader your school and community need. It is not about collecting certificates or logging PD hours. It is about closing the gap between the demands of the role and the preparation most principals actually receive.

That gap is real. A national study found that nearly 1 in 10 principals leave their schools each year. Behind those numbers are leaders who entered the role passionate and capable, but unprepared for the weight of daily decisions. They were managing crises, supervising instruction, fielding parent complaints, and navigating politics without the coaching or tools to do it well. Over time, the strain outpaced their support, and they left (National Center for Education Statistics, 2023).

That is what makes ongoing professional development essential. It is the process of adding tools to your leadership toolbox, learning practices that make the job sustainable, and having spaces where you can reflect, ask questions, and learn from others who understand the challenges. This kind of preparation equips principals to make better decisions, handle conflict with confidence, and stay connected to their purpose amidst pressure.

When a principal is equipped with the right tools and support, the effects ripple outward to teachers, families, and students. That is the real purpose of professional growth: not simply to help leaders endure, but to ensure entire school communities can thrive.

The Weight That Won't Wait

Principals often shoulder numerous responsibilities, not out of a desire for control, but from a deep sense of care. They do it because their dream is big. Initially, the demanding schedule and significant responsibilities appear manageable. It's common to spend evenings away from home, miss family occasions, and respond to emails late at night and again before dawn. Lunches are skipped, and the calendar remains perpetually full. This intense pace might seem effective because tasks are completed, and the principal is consistently present. However, beneath the surface, an imbalance is silently growing.

That imbalance shows itself in subtle ways at first. It starts with the "Sunday scaries" that begin with the thought of returning to work on Monday, the head cold that lingers for weeks, and waking up at 3:00 a.m. to run through tomorrow's problems. These aren't perks of the job. They're alarms, warning that too much weight is resting on one person. Sacrifice will always be part of leadership, but when those moments become the norm instead of the exception, the work no longer feels like a noble calling, but rather a cycle of exhaustion where it's impossible to catch up.

This is the weight that won't wait. And it isn't just about tasks. It's the responsibility of shaping the lives of hundreds of children. It's guiding the careers of the adults in the building. It's carrying the burden of safety every single day. It's meeting the expectations of parents, districts, and state and federal requirements. None of these pressures pauses until leaders are ready. The weight keeps coming, and it lands on the principal first.

Strengths-Based Leadership

When principals think about their own development, the focus often drifts toward weaknesses. "I need to get better at discipline." "I'm not good with budgets." "I struggle with delegation." Those are real areas to improve, but if growth is only about fixing what you lack, leadership quickly becomes discouraging.

The most effective leaders flip that script. They start with their strengths and lead from what they do best. Gallup's research on strengths-based leadership is clear (Rath and Conchie 27). Teams perform better and stay longer when their leaders recognize and utilize their own strengths. In schools, this means recognizing the areas where you bring energy and clarity, whether it's casting vision, building relationships, designing systems, or coaching instruction, and leaning into those as your leadership advantage.

This doesn't excuse blind spots or weaknesses. It means you stop wasting energy trying to be someone you are not and instead surround yourself with people who can do what you cannot. If your strength lies in relationships, you may benefit from having a process-minded colleague by your side. If your strength is systems, you will need others who naturally connect and inspire. Leadership is not about being well-rounded as an individual; it's about building a well-rounded team.

When Wendy Kopp founded *Teach For America*, she was only twenty-two. She had no formal leadership training, no organizational management background, and no roadmap for scaling a national nonprofit. What she did have was vision. She believed that talented young teachers could make a difference in under-resourced schools, and she could rally others to believe it too (Kopp, 2011).

However, vision alone was insufficient to run an organization that grew from a college campus idea into a movement spanning thousands of teachers. Kopp quickly discovered that the operational side (budgets, compliance, and systems) was not her strength. Instead of pretending she could master every detail, she named it. She leaned fully into what she did best: casting vision, inspiring people, and relentlessly advocating for kids. For the rest, she built a team of leaders whose strengths balanced her weaknesses. Strategists, operators, and managers took on what she could not.

Her honesty about her limits didn't diminish her leadership; it strengthened it. Teach For America flourished because it stopped trying to be everything and instead created a culture where people's unique gifts mattered. Her story proves a truth that every principal needs to hear: Effective leadership does not require mastering every skill or area. True strength comes from understanding your unique gifts, openly acknowledging your limits, and building a team that complements your weaknesses. Wendy Kopp's journey with Teach For America shows that embracing this truth leads to stronger leadership and greater impact.

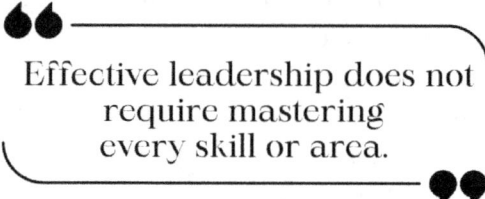

Effective leadership does not require mastering every skill or area.

The point is not to label yourself. It is to understand how you are wired. Pay attention to the work that gives you energy and the work that drains you. Notice the moments when time moves quickly because you are in your lane, and the moments you avoid because they leave you frustrated. That awareness is not self-indulgent. It is data for leadership.

Use that data to make three choices. First, lead from the places where you bring your best. Second, invite others to stand beside you where you are not strong. Third, choose one or two skills you will learn this year because your role requires them. Strengths-based leadership doesn't give anyone a free pass to get out of learning and growing. It shows you where to maximize your natural talents, where to partner with others whose strengths cover your gaps, and where targeted development will actually make a difference.

When principals lead from their strengths, acknowledge their weaknesses, and invite others to step into the gaps, staff notice and are encouraged. Support shows up sooner because responsibilities are shared, and teachers know exactly who to turn to for help. When teachers see their principal lean into strengths and admit areas for growth, they feel safe to do the same. Staff become more willing to share where they need support, ask for professional development, and own both their strengths and weaknesses. That kind of honesty builds trust, and it is that trust that makes the school a place where people want to stay.

Reflection: The Practice That Builds Self-Awareness

Aristotle famously said, "Knowing yourself is the beginning of all wisdom." Leading authentically and effectively starts with a deep awareness of your unique strengths, values, and patterns. This awareness isn't gained through a single moment or one-time assessment; it is cultivated continuously

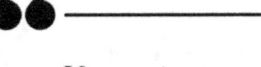

Knowing yourself is the beginning of all wisdom.

through reflection. Reflection is the intentional practice of pausing to thoughtfully examine your actions, decisions, and emotions. Through this ongoing process, you gain meaningful insight into what's working well and what needs adjustment, ultimately building the self-awareness foundational to strong, grounded leadership.

Regular reflection builds self-awareness, the foundation of emotional intelligence. It helps leaders manage stress, respond thoughtfully to challenges, and maintain authenticity in their leadership. Without reflection, principals stay stuck in reaction mode, moving from one crisis to the next without learning from the pattern.

Reflection fosters continuous learning by helping leaders recognize patterns, avoid repeating mistakes, and adapt their strategies to serve their teams better. It cultivates humility and openness, encouraging leaders to seek feedback and embrace growth opportunities. When you reflect on a difficult conversation, you might notice you rushed to solve the problem instead of listening. When you reflect on a decision that backfired, you might see where assumptions led you astray. That awareness creates the opportunity to do better next time.

Reflective practice supports resilience. Leaders who process setbacks constructively rather than reactively recover faster and lead with more clarity. Action without reflection leads to repetition. Reflection after action leads to growth. When leaders take time to reflect on what worked and what didn't, they turn experience into wisdom, improving their effectiveness and aligning their actions with their values for long-term impact.

The most effective reflection happens on a consistent rhythm. Daily reflection can be brief, taking just a few minutes at the end of the day to ask, "What went well? What challenges arose? What did I learn?" Weekly reflection allows for deeper processing during a planning or review session, assessing progress on goals, and planning adjustments. Monthly or quarterly reflection provides space to evaluate broader patterns, leadership effectiveness, and strategic direction, often supported by gathering feedback and data.

Regular reflection prevents feeling overwhelmed and making quick reactive decisions by creating time to learn, course-correct, and celebrate growth. It's better to reflect routinely, even in small doses, than sporadically with long gaps.

Leaders who lead themselves well through reflection model the mindset of growth and intentionality they wish to see in others. This influences organizational culture, promoting a learning environment where adapting and evolving are valued. When staff see their principal pause, reflect, and adjust, they feel permission to do the same.

Normalize reflection by sharing your own insights openly and using team meetings as brief moments for collective reflection. Providing dedicated time, even just five to ten minutes, helps make it a regular practice without overwhelming staff with extra steps.

Connection is the Game-Changer

Leadership is hard. Principals second-guess every decision, knowing they'll never please everyone. They have to learn how to manage what to share and what not to share, who to include, and who to keep out. They wrestle with when to collaborate and when to just make a call. They carry the weight of knowing their decisions impact many lives. And they're expected not to take any of it personally.

That weight leads to isolation. Research shows that principals often experience emotional isolation because of the unique responsibilities they carry alone, which can lead to loneliness, stress, burnout, and diminished job satisfaction (Bauer et al., 2021; CASEL, 2024). Isolation affects persistence in the role and increases intentions to leave. But when principals realize they are not alone in facing these challenges, it alleviates the emotional burden and improves their sense of connection and support.

In my work with principals, I often hear relief when someone says, "I thought I was the only one dealing with this." That simple moment of recognition changes everything. The problems don't disappear, but the leader no longer feels isolated. Connection through professional networks, coaching, and genuine friendship reduces feelings of isolation by fostering shared experience. Recognition of common challenges bolsters principals' capacity to lead effectively.

We learn from each other. Iron sharpens iron. When principals engage in meaningful connections with peers, mentors, and coaches, they gain emotional support and practical guidance that improve their decision-making and stress management. This connectedness fosters a sense of belonging, reducing feelings of loneliness and burnout. When principals sit with peers or coaches and process their real challenges, two things happen. First, they gain perspective. Another leader's question or insight helps them see their situation from a different angle. Second, they gain confidence. They walk away with new language to use, a strategy to try, and the assurance that they are not off track.

> "When principals engage in meaningful connections with peers, mentors, and coaches, they gain emotional support and practical guidance that improve their decision-making and stress management."

This professional exchange is a lifeline. Explaining your own leadership approach to a peer sharpens your clarity immediately. Listening to a colleague's challenges broadens your perspective and prepares you for future obstacles. This shared learning fosters the trust and external accountability necessary to sustain your drive and resilience in the long term, keeping you moving forward even when the work gets difficult.

Connection also extends to your staff. Modeling growth as a leader sets the tone for the entire school culture. When staff see their principal still learning, still curious, and still willing to improve, it motivates them to pursue their own development. A principal who shares what they're reading, admits where they're struggling, and asks for feedback creates a culture where growth is expected and celebrated.

Shared learning opportunities amplify this effect. When principals invite staff into book studies, collaborative professional development, or learning walks where everyone observes and learns together, growth becomes a team effort. Professional development and collaborative learning opportunities rooted in connection contribute to improved teacher retention, school climate, and student achievement. Teachers who learn alongside their principal feel valued and empowered. They bring forward new ideas, ask for feedback, and admit where they need support. The culture shifts from one of silence and survival to one of collaboration and growth.

Creating a rhythm of connection transforms leadership from a solitary burden into a shared mission with greater impact. No principal should lead in isolation. Connection with peers, mentors, or coaches turns leadership from a lonely struggle into a shared journey. Seek out your circle, find your tribe, and invest in yourself. Learn and grow together because connection is what turns professional growth into purpose-driven leadership.

Finding the Rhythm

Understanding the weight of leadership is one thing, but executing a sustainable rhythm to manage that weight is a critical element of leadership success. School life runs in seasons. August and May stretch long and heavy. That reality cannot be changed. Balance appears when leaders guard recovery during the months that allow it. Winter break, spring break, and summer are recovery periods to be protected, not filled with additional work projects.

One helpful framework is the **2x2x2 rhythm**, which protects time at every level of leadership:

- **2 Days a Week:** Free of meetings, reserved for walkthroughs, planning, and proactive work.

- **2 Hours a Day:** Blocked for preparation and reflection, treated like any vital meeting, and protected from interruptions.

- **2 Weeks a Year:** Set aside for retreats or deep work away from daily demands to reset priorities and strengthen team alignment.

- **2 Months a Year:** Protected for renewal, system building, and reset. Summer or slower stretches give leaders the space to prepare for the next heavy season.

This rhythm only works if it is scheduled. Each block must be treated as a non-negotiable appointment, requiring the same level of attention as an essential meeting. If the time is not reserved, it disappears under the weight of the urgent. The 2x2x2x2 rhythm moves balance from a vague idea to a concrete structure. It helps leaders protect their time, hours, days, and weeks, allowing them to sustain the work long term.

The weight of this role cannot be ignored, but with simple structures, wise delegation, and steady rhythms, it can be manageable, and even enjoyable. These shifts create the margin principals need to lead with clarity and stay connected to the purpose of the work.

Investing in Yourself

Leading yourself is the most challenging leadership work you will do. As Bill George writes in True North (2007), "The hardest person to lead is yourself." Yet this is where effective leadership begins. When leaders invest in developing self-discipline, emotional intelligence, and clarity of purpose, they build the resilience needed to handle complex challenges and lead others effectively.

Leading yourself well is a holistic practice that encompasses nurturing your physical, mental, emotional, and spiritual well-being to sustain effective leadership over time. Physically, self-leadership involves ensuring you get enough rest, exercise, and proper nutrition to maintain high energy and focus. Mentally, it requires sharpening your thinking, engaging in continuous learning, and cultivating positive thought patterns that promote motivation and problem-solving. Emotionally, it is about understanding and regulating your feelings while fostering supportive relationships that reinforce resilience. Spiritually, it means connecting with your deeper values and purpose, which provides meaning and authenticity in your leadership journey.

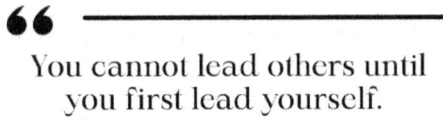

> You cannot lead others until you first lead yourself.

As John C. Maxwell writes in The Self-Aware Leader (2021), "You cannot lead others until you first lead yourself. You can lead yourself at your best only if you invest in yourself first." Investing in yourself means protecting time for practices that deepen self-awareness. This includes reflection through journaling or mindfulness, which helps leaders process experiences, track progress, and develop intentional action plans for improvement. It means seeking out coaching or peer circles that challenge your thinking and expand your perspective. It means continuously developing your understanding of your strengths, weaknesses, values, motivations, and the impact you have on others. This self-knowledge enables leaders to act with clarity, authenticity, and resilience.

Principals who stop investing in themselves start making reactive decisions instead of strategic ones. They lose sight of why they took the job. They burn out not because the work is hard, but because they have stopped building capacity to handle it. Growth is the necessary commitment you make to yourself, keeping your personal passion ignited so you can lead your entire community toward their potential.

Scholars like Warren Bennis (Bennis, 2009) call self-mastery the heart of leadership. Self-leadership fosters a culture of growth, trust, and shared purpose in teams and organizations. The principals who stay in leadership and thrive are not the ones who work harder. They are the ones who invest in themselves consistently. They know that leading others well begins with leading themselves well. They understand that their growth shapes the culture of their school. This foundation of leading yourself well sustains leaders through challenges and empowers them to inspire and guide others with confidence.

Investing in yourself is the critical first step toward sustained, effective leadership. When you lead from your strengths, reflect regularly on your decisions and growth, build sustainable rhythms that protect time for renewal, connect with peers who sharpen your thinking, and invest in your whole self physically, mentally, emotionally, and spiritually, you build the capacity to lead well over the long haul.

Growing Your Staff: The Principal's Role in Professional Development

Now that we've talked about leading yourself well, let's turn to the other half of the Professional Growth Pillar: developing your staff. Purpose-driven principals understand that their own growth is only half the equation. The other half is creating the conditions where every person in the building can grow, too.

For years, I sat through professional development that felt like a waste of time. We'd gather in the library, listen to someone talk at us for two hours, and leave with a binder we'd never open again. I remember thinking, "If this is what PD feels like for me, what must it feel like for my teachers?" That question changed how I approached professional development after becoming a principal.

I knew I wanted something different. Not just better workshops, but a complete shift in how we thought about growth. I wanted professional development that honored the fact that my teachers were professionals with different strengths, different needs, and in various stages in their careers. I wanted support staff to feel valued and invested in, not forgotten. And I wanted everyone to take ownership of their own learning instead of sitting passively through something I told them they had to do.

So, I restructured how we approached professional development entirely. We broke teachers into grade-level teams for targeted, relevant learning specific to their teaching. Once a month, we came together as an all-staff to deepen our understanding of our mission, vision, and core values, and to train everyone on new initiatives and platforms we were implementing schoolwide.

Just as students benefit from differentiated instruction, teachers and staff benefit from professional development tailored to their individual needs. But too often, we treat professional development like one-size-fits-all. Everyone sits through the same workshop, whether they've already mastered the content or have never seen it before. That approach wastes time, breeds resentment, and rarely changes anything.

> " Just as students benefit from differentiated instruction, teachers and staff benefit from professional development tailored to their individual needs. "

One year, I gamified professional development. I provided access to online learning platforms where teachers and staff could choose what they wanted to learn based on their own goals and interests. They created their own individualized learning plans. For every tier of videos they watched and completed, they earned rewards: books, duty-free passes, lunch where they could choose their own takeout, coffee gift cards, and the top tier earned a full day off. I posted the dashboard in my monthly newsletter so everyone could see the progress.

What surprised me most was watching staff blow past the highest tier. Some kept going, learning far beyond what I'd incentivized, simply because they were engaged and curious. That's when I realized the real power wasn't in the rewards. It was in giving them ownership. When people choose their own learning, they don't stop when the requirements are met. They keep growing because they want to.

Research confirms this approach. High-quality professional development reduces teacher attrition by 25% (Learning Policy Institute, 2017). Districts that offered teachers choice in their training saw 80% report above-average retention, and those using personalized professional

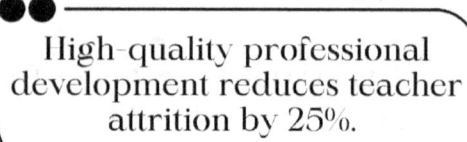

High-quality professional development reduces teacher attrition by 25%.

development systems were eight times more likely to report easier hiring and stronger staff stability (Frontline Education, 2025). Furthermore, teachers who find professional development "very useful" are far more likely to stay in the profession (Economic Policy Institute, 2019). High-quality PD reduces teacher attrition by 25% (Learning Policy Institute, 2017).

Professional development isn't just for teachers. Every role in a school deserves growth opportunities specific to their work. Paraprofessionals need behavior support strategies. Custodians benefit from learning efficient work order systems. Cafeteria workers grow from training on nutrition and food safety. Office staff need development on student information systems. Secretaries benefit from customer service training and managing difficult conversations. When professional development speaks directly to the work people actually do, it's relevant. And when it's relevant, people lean in.

Like most principals, I asked staff at the beginning and end of every year what professional development they wanted. But asking isn't enough. If we're going to ask, we must show we care by connecting them to what they've identified. Sometimes that meant I found the conferences or workshops. Other times, I encouraged staff to find a conference or training they'd like to attend and bring it to me. Some wanted to visit other schools to see different approaches in action. Whatever they identified, I worked to make it happen and gave them time to attend. One practice worth considering is to sit with your teachers during professional development. Take notes, ask questions, and learn alongside them. When you understand what they're learning, you can better support them in the classroom afterward. You can connect what they wanted to learn to on-the-job coaching, reference specific strategies they're trying, and provide targeted feedback in the moment when it matters most.

Usually, what the staff and faculty ask for in development aligns with what you've already seen they need. But when they identify it themselves, they're invested in a way they never would be if you told them what they needed. Their growth becomes personal, not prescribed. When you follow through by truly seeing their request and finding the resources, you send a clear message: your voice matters, your growth is a priority, and we're invested in helping you get there. But if you're not willing to do that work, don't ask. Asking and not following through does more damage than never asking at all.

Conferences and workshops are vital, but they can't replace the most powerful professional development, which doesn't happen in a workshop at all. It happens in the classroom, in the moment, with real students. When I was a teacher, one of my biggest pet peeves was receiving general emails addressing someone's mistake as a reminder to everyone, instead of the principal having a conversation with the person who needed it. When I became a principal, I made it a point to have honest conversations. Without the conversation, I couldn't understand the context. Maybe that teacher was overwhelmed and needed support. Perhaps something was going on at home. The conversation creates an opportunity to coach, listen, and support.

When principals differentiate professional learning and align it with collective goals, they create an environment where everyone feels empowered rather than overwhelmed. Differentiated professional development supports efficacy, increases retention, and improves student outcomes. But differentiation alone isn't enough. Professional development must also align with the school's mission and vision. If your mission emphasizes student-centered learning but your professional development focuses on compliance and test prep, there's a disconnect. This will confuse your staff, leading them to question your actual values.

The national teacher retention averages 78%, but schools with personalized professional development see retention rates climb to 85%. Teachers in personalized programs report 76% higher job satisfaction (Darling-Hammond et al., 2017). Personalized, meaningful professional development isn't just a growth strategy. It's a retention strategy that strengthens teaching quality, staff culture, and organizational stability.

Purpose-driven principals know that professional growth for staff begins with them. When you invest in their development with the same intentionality you invest in your own, you build a culture where learning is the norm, not the exception. And that culture transforms schools.

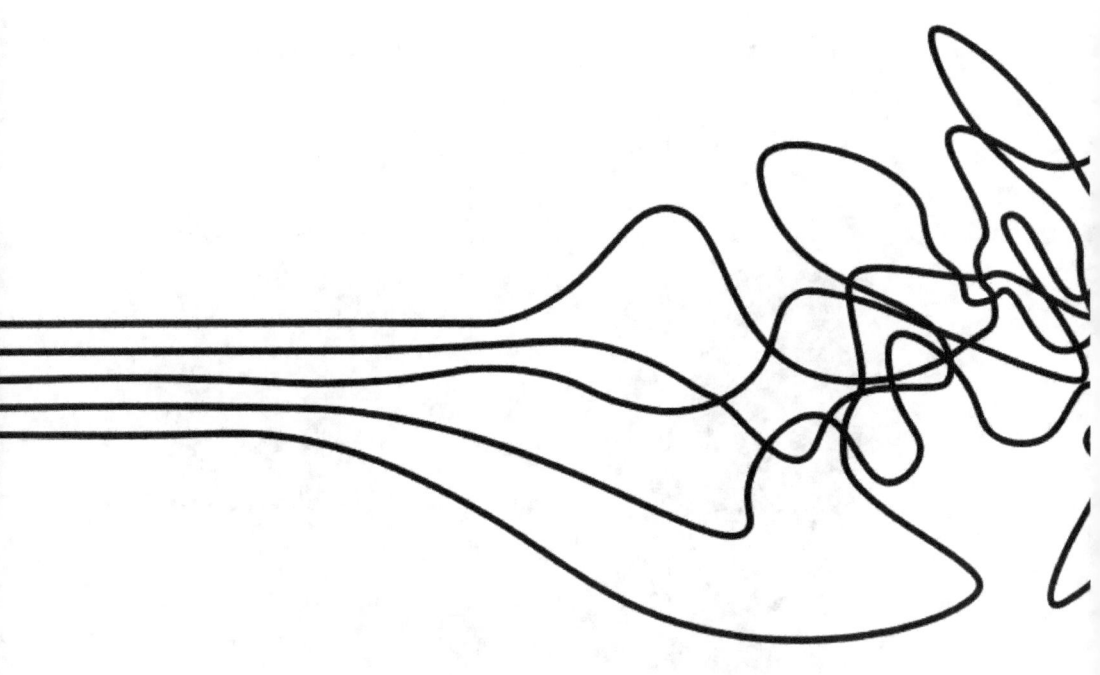

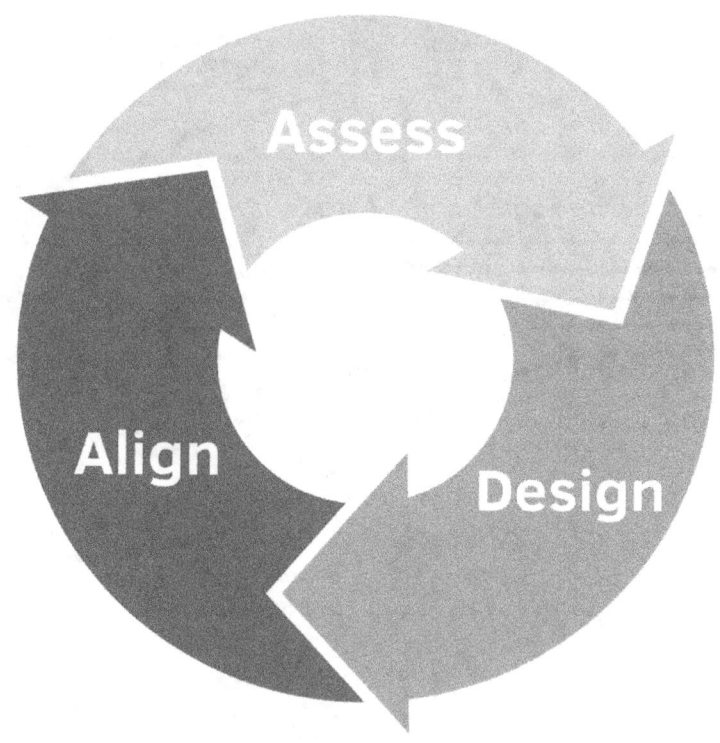

CHAPTER 6

The Assess-Design-Align Cycle: How to Keep it Alive

The purpose foundation and four pillars (People, Pedagogy, Processes, and Professional Growth) create the structure for a thriving school. But structure alone doesn't guarantee success. Schools are living systems. They shift as staff change, as student needs evolve, as new challenges emerge. A rhythm for continuously evaluating and refining the work keeps even the strongest foundation from weakening and the most intentional work from losing focus.

The Assess-Design-Align cycle is the strategic process I use when partnering with school leaders to build the thriving, purpose-driven school they envision.

1. During the **Assess** phase, we conduct a comprehensive discovery audit centered on the Purpose Driven Principal Framework. This systematic review uses surveys, focus groups, and observations to identify clear gaps, strengths, and opportunities for growth within the current system using the SWOT analysis.

2. During the **Design** phase, we move from diagnosis to creation. All strategies created here intentionally address the gaps and leverage the opportunities identified in the audit. This involves revising or creating foundational documents, such as the Mission and Vision (if necessary),

mapping out intentional celebrations of wins throughout the school year, and developing specific strategies to close the identified gaps. This is where we create the beliefs, mindsets, and practices needed to move forward, setting SMART goals that measure progress and help accomplish the school's vision.

3. During the **Align** phase, we bring unity to the work by ensuring every department, stakeholder, policy, and practice moves in the same direction toward those goals and aligns with the school's core values, mission, and vision.

Together, these three phases ensure the work of continuous evaluation and refinement remains systematic, focused, and effective. Too many schools operate on assumptions. Leaders believe communication is working because no one complains. They assume staff are aligned because meetings happen. They think systems are strong because routines exist. Assessment challenges those assumptions. Design creates solutions. Alignment embeds those solutions into the school's systems.

The Assess-Design-Align cycle is how purpose-driven principals lead with clarity instead of guesswork. It provides the structure for data-informed decision-making, strategic planning, and sustained improvement.

This chapter walks you through each step of the cycle, shows you how to make it a rhythm rather than a one-time event, and helps you see how it keeps your school focused, responsive, and growing.

Why the Cycle Matters

The purpose foundation and four pillars create the structure for a thriving school. But the structure requires continuous attention. The Assess-Design-Align cycle is how you keep that foundation and those pillars strong.

Principals work incredibly hard. But many still feel stuck. They launch initiatives that fade by midyear. They announce priorities that staff can't recall a month later. They make decisions based on what they think is happening, only to discover later that reality looked very different. This occurs when leaders operate on assumptions instead of evidence.

Silence is not proof of health. Some of the deepest problems in a school are the ones nobody mentions until they've already caused damage.

I've seen principals gather pages of survey results, walkthrough data, and staff feedback, then file them away. The data was clear. The needs were real. But nothing happened. Not because they didn't care, but because they didn't know where to start. Twenty different issues surfaced, and they couldn't decide which to tackle first. Or they got buried under daily demands and never returned to the data. Or they felt paralyzed by the feedback and avoided the hard conversations it required.

Meanwhile, teachers stop participating. I've heard them say, "I'm not going to fill out one more survey because nothing ever changes. Why take the time to share my thoughts, be honest, if they aren't going to do anything about it?" Assessment without change creates cynicism. Knowing the problems doesn't solve them.

The cycle matters because it moves leadership from reactive to strategic. Reactive leaders solve the same problems repeatedly. Strategic leaders address root causes. Reactive leaders chase trends. Strategic leaders stay focused on their mission. Reactive leaders exhaust staff with constant change. Strategic leaders build momentum through consistency.

When you make Assess-Design-Align a rhythm, you stop guessing. You lead from evidence. You prioritize based on what the assessment shows instead of reacting to the loudest voice. You know whether your efforts are producing results because you measure them.

Schools that skip this cycle repeat the same problems year after year. They work harder but wonder why nothing improves.

Schools that embrace this cycle see progress compound. Small wins turn into sustained improvement. The work gets easier because everyone knows where to focus their energy.

The difference isn't effort. It's rhythm. The Assess-Design-Align cycle is that rhythm.

Step One: Assess — Looking Honestly at What's True

Assessment in this cycle isn't an annual event. It's a strategic pause that happens before every major decision, initiative, or pivot. The question isn't "Should we assess?" It's "What exactly are we assessing, and what will we do with what we find?"

Here's what most principals miss: they assess everything and act on nothing. Or they assess one thing and miss the systemic issues beneath the surface. Strategic assessment is targeted, connects to the mission, vision, core values, and all four pillars. It answers one question: **Where is the gap between what we say and what's actually happening?**

Before You Assess: Four Questions That Focus the Work

Strategic assessment starts with clarity. Before you send one survey or schedule one focus group, answer these four questions:

1. **What's the real question?** "Do our staff understand how our mission should shape daily instruction?" or "Can families articulate what makes our school different?"
2. **Which part of the framework are we examining?** Purpose? People? Pedagogy? Processes? Professional Growth? This keeps you from assessing random things that don't connect to your goal.
3. **What evidence will actually answer this?** Be specific about which tools will give you the clearest picture.

4. **Are we ready to act on what we find?** If you're not prepared to respond to uncomfortable truths, don't assess yet. Asking without acting kills trust faster than not asking at all.

The Two Data Streams You Can't Skip

Hard Data (Quantitative): Numbers don't lie, but they don't tell the whole story. Use them to spot patterns—such as survey results, attendance trends, discipline data, walkthrough tallies, and other measurable indicators.

Soft Data (Qualitative): This is where you learn the "why" behind the numbers. Hallway conversations, focus groups, exit slips after professional development, and what you notice when you're simply present all reveal what people won't write on surveys.

The power is in the combination. If 80% of staff say they feel supported (quantitative) but three separate conversations reveal they don't know who to ask for help (qualitative), you've found your gap.

Assess: The Questions That Matter

Don't assess everything about everything. Assess the specific things that tell you whether your pillars are holding or cracking.

Purpose:

- Can staff recite the mission?
- Do students know what your values are? (Ask them. Their answers will surprise you.)
- When you observe a classroom or meeting, can you see the mission in action?

People:

- Who doesn't feel safe here? (You won't find this in a survey. You'll find it when you pay attention to who's quiet, who's isolated, who's missing.)

- Where are relationships breaking down? (Staff to staff? Staff to students? School to families?)
- Do people trust leadership enough to tell the truth? (If every survey is glowing, you're not getting honesty.)

Pedagogy:

- What does "good teaching" mean here? (If five different teachers give five different answers, you haven't aligned this yet.)
- Are students learning, or just complying? (Walkthrough data: Are they engaged or just quiet?)
- What does student work actually show? (Bring work samples to meetings.)

Processes:

- What question do you get asked more than once a week? (That's a missing or broken process.)
- What takes way longer than it should? (That's an inefficient system.)
- What do people avoid because it's confusing? (That's an unclear procedure.)

Professional Growth:

- Are teachers learning, or just sitting through PD? (Survey after every training: useful or not?)
- Who's growing and who's stagnating?
- Is growth aligned with the mission, or random? (If your mission is student-centered learning but your PD is all about test prep, there's your gap.)
- Are you, as the principal, still learning? (When's the last time you read something that changed how you lead? When did you last ask for feedback on your own leadership?)
- Are you leading yourself well?

Assessment is the essential diagnostic step that enables all subsequent actions. It demands rigor, honesty, and the courage to involve others in naming what's true. When you assess well, you gather the evidence

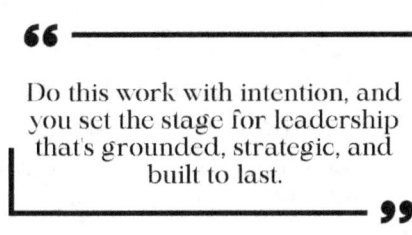

> Do this work with intention, and you set the stage for leadership that's grounded, strategic, and built to last.

needed to design solutions that actually fit your school, not someone else's playbook. You create clarity about where the foundation is strong and where the pillars need attention. Do this work with intention, and you set the stage for leadership that's grounded, strategic, and built to last.

Step Two: Design — Turning Evidence into Action

This is where most schools stall. They gather feedback, identify problems, acknowledge gaps, and then nothing changes. Surveys sit in folders. Walkthrough data gets filed away. Staff meetings end with "we need to work on communication," but no one defines what that actually means or who owns it.

Design is the bridge between knowing and doing. It's where insights from assessment become concrete strategies, plans, and interventions tailored to your school's unique context and needs.

The Design Trap

The mistake most principals make is trying to design solutions for everything that the assessment revealed. Twenty problems surface, so they create twenty initiatives. Staff get overwhelmed. No initiative receives the focus it needs to succeed. Burnout follows.

The Design Process

Effective design follows a clear sequence:

1. **Narrow the Focus:** Choose two or three priorities based on patterns from assessment, not isolated complaints. Select the highest-impact areas that align with your mission. If everything is a priority, nothing is a priority.

> If everything is a priority, then nothing is a priority.

2. **Set Clear Goals:** Vague goals produce vague results. "Improve communication" doesn't tell anyone what success looks like. Instead, answer four questions:

- What specific change or outcome are we seeking?
- Who is responsible for leading and supporting this change?
- How will success be measured, and what evidence will show progress?
- What is the timeline for initial progress checks and final evaluation?

3. **Involve Stakeholders:** Design fails when it's done in isolation. A principal who creates a plan alone and announces it to staff guarantees resistance. People support what they help create.

Collaborate with teachers, staff, families, and community members throughout the design process, not just at the end. When stakeholders co-create the solution, they carry responsibility for making it work. This inclusion fosters ownership and increases the likelihood of successful implementation.

4. **Develop Evidence-Based Strategies:** Craft strategies that directly address the prioritized needs assessment revealed. This might involve curricular changes, professional development plans, resource allocation, or policy adjustments. Base your design on well-researched best practices, then adapt them to your local conditions and context.

The specific interventions will look different in every school because they must be tailored to your unique mission, context, and community. A targeted coaching program with peer observations might be precisely what one school needs for its pedagogy. Monthly staff circles for honest conversation might rebuild trust in another school's culture. A redesigned onboarding system might solve process gaps for a third school. The strategy matters less than whether it fits your purpose and addresses what the assessment revealed.

5. **Plan for Resources and Sustainability:** Good design answers the question: What do we need to make this work?

Too many initiatives die after the first year because they depend on one person's energy or on a grant that has expired. Design must plan for sustainability. Ask: If the person leading this leaves, does the system collapse? If the answer is yes, the design isn't sustainable yet.

Design Strengthens Every Pillar

Whether you're addressing gaps in instructional practices, rebuilding trust among staff, streamlining unclear processes, or developing leadership capacity, the design process remains the same: narrow the focus, set clear goals, involve stakeholders, develop evidence-based strategies, plan for resources, and build for sustainability.

Step Three: Align — From Plans to Practice

Alignment is the process of ensuring that all parts of your school (its people, strategies, systems, structures, and daily practices) are consistently coordinated and working toward the same overarching goals and mission. It's the phase that transforms well-designed plans into lived realities through coordinated and purposeful action.

Alignment brings everything together. Assessment reveals the gaps, strengths, and opportunities. Design creates the SMART goals, strategies, and action plans. The Align step ensures that every decision, resource, and daily practice moves your school toward what you created during the design phase and aligns with your mission, vision, and core values.

What Alignment Actually Means

Alignment means synchronizing efforts and resources so that every action supports the strategic objectives you defined during the design phase. It creates clarity around roles and responsibilities so that all individuals understand how their work fits into the bigger goals. It establishes shared accountability through monitoring progress and providing feedback loops. It embeds the mission, vision, and values into the school's daily operations, culture, and communication.

Alignment bridges the gap between strategy and execution. It helps your school move from ambition to measurable results. It creates a unified, coherent organization where every component pulls in the same direction to achieve common goals sustainably and effectively.

Using Mission, Vision, and Values as Filters

Every school leader makes hundreds of decisions each week. Which professional development to fund? Which discipline policy to revise? Which new program to adopt? Which meeting to prioritize? Filter every decision through your mission, vision, and core values. Before saying yes to anything, ask: Does this reflect our mission? Does this move us toward our vision? Does this embody our core values? If the answer is no, don't do it. If the answer is unclear, pause and clarify before moving forward.

This filter keeps your SMART goals from becoming disconnected initiatives. It ensures that the strategies you designed stay rooted in who you are as a school, not just what you want to accomplish.

Conducting Alignment Audits

Regular alignment audits help you find where words and actions diverge. Walk through your building with fresh eyes. Do classroom practices reflect the instructional vision you designed? Do staff interactions reflect the culture you committed to building? Do your policies support or undermine the mission?

Review your calendar and budget. Where does your time go? Where does your money go? If those don't align with your stated priorities, you've found a gap.

Ask your staff and students. Can they articulate the mission? Do they see it in action? Their answers reveal the truth.

Creating a Feedback Loop

Consistent alignment requires regular assessment. Create regular opportunities for assessment, such as monthly leadership team check-ins, quarterly staff pulse checks, and annual full-cycle reviews that ask questions like: Are our actions matching our priorities? Do you see our mission reflected in what we're doing? Where are we aligned? Where have we shifted?

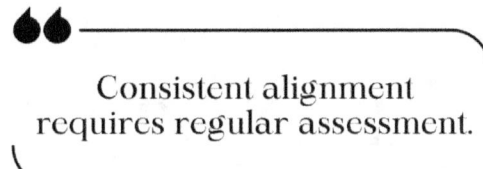

Consistent alignment requires regular assessment.

When misalignment surfaces, address it quickly. Name it, own it, and design a way to realign it.

This feedback loop connects back to the assessment. You're continuously gathering evidence about whether your aligned actions are producing the results you designed. When they're not, you assess why, redesign as needed, and realign. The cycle continues.

Leaders stop guessing and start leading from evidence. Staff stop feeling whiplashed by random initiatives because the work has focus and coherence. Students and families experience a school that knows what it stands for and lives it consistently.

The Assess-Design-Align cycle is the strategic rhythm that keeps your Purpose Foundation and Four Pillars strong. Assessment reveals the truth; Design creates the roadmap; and Alignment ensures unity in execution. Making this a consistent, sustained practice is how you lead with enhanced clarity, focus, and evidence, ensuring your school is always moving toward what's possible. This sustained commitment is the ultimate definition of purpose-driven leadership..

CHAPTER 7

Called to Lead, Anchored in Purpose

Pause for a moment.

Think back to the day you accepted this role, or even further back, to the moment you first imagined yourself as a principal. What did you see?

Maybe you saw yourself walking into the building each morning feeling pride and joy. You had a smile on your face, filled with energy to tackle the day's challenges. You envisioned students walking with confidence, knowing they belonged. Or perhaps you saw yourself in those critical moments when a student made a poor choice and you'd have the kind of conversation that helped them see who they were becoming, discover their purpose, and truly understand that they were seen, loved, and valued. You saw student leaders stepping up to run initiatives they cared about. Peer mediators resolving conflicts with wisdom. Fifth graders reading to kindergarteners. Hallways where kindness flowed naturally because character was modeled, not mandated.

You might have imagined parents who trusted you completely. They'd drop their children off knowing they were safe, that learning would be joyful and challenging, and that their child's curiosity would be protected and nurtured for life. When concerns arose, you'd meet them as partners, working together for the good of their child. Parents would volunteer in classrooms because they wanted to be part of what was happening. They'd attend events not out of obligation, but out of excitement. They'd share stories on social media about the teacher who changed their child's life or the moment their student finally felt seen. They'd tell their neighbors about the good happening inside your building.

And what about your teachers? You may have seen a team that rallied around a shared mission. New initiatives were embraced with enthusiasm. They'd join the vision without needing extensive convincing, owning their classrooms and serving with joy. Maybe you envisioned them thanking you, cheering you on, and expressing gratitude for the leadership and direction you provided. You'd walk into their classrooms not to evaluate, but to encourage. You'd sit with them during planning periods and have meaningful conversations about their growth and their students. You'd leave notes on their desks that reminded them why their work mattered. You'd publicly celebrate their wins and privately support them through challenges. Staff meetings would feel productive, not draining. Professional development would spark real growth, not check compliance boxes.

Or maybe you envisioned a community that showed up to volunteer and serve. Fundraisers that exceeded goals because people believed in what you were building. Events packed with families. Local businesses are eager to partner because they can see the impact you are making. The bakery is donating treats for student celebrations. The bookstore sponsors reading challenges. The senior center is collaborating on intergenerational projects. They launched joint initiatives that strengthened both the school and the neighborhood. A community that didn't just support from a distance but proudly participated in the mission.

That was the dream.

And then you started the job.

When the Dream Meets Reality

Somewhere between bus schedules, behavior referrals, and the weight of constant decision-making, the dream got buried. The work became about managing what was right in front of you, and the intentional pieces kept waiting for a quieter day that never came.

You started questioning yourself. Maybe you weren't cut out for this. Maybe other principals had something you didn't. Perhaps you were in over your head.

> **"** You were chosen for this role because someone saw what you had to offer. They saw your heart for students. They recognized your ability to connect with people. They trusted your judgment. They believed you could lead. **"**

But that voice telling you you're not enough? Don't listen to it.

You were chosen for this role because someone saw what you had to offer. They saw your heart for students. They recognized your ability to connect with people. They trusted your judgment. They believed you could lead.

And they were right.

You Have What It Takes

Leaders don't have to have all the answers. They ask the right questions. They don't have to be perfect. They show up and stay present. They don't do everything themselves. They build systems and develop people, so the work becomes sustainable.

You don't need to be someone else. The world doesn't need another version of the principal down the street or the leader you read about in a book. Your school needs you. With your gifts. With your perspective. With your voice.

The doubt you feel? It means you care. It means you understand the weight of what you carry. Leaders who never question themselves often lack the humility required to lead well. Your awareness of what you don't know makes you teachable. Your willingness to grow makes you effective.

The Mindset Shifts That Change Everything

Leadership challenges you to see yourself, your work, and your people differently than you did before. The beliefs that helped you succeed as a teacher or assistant principal won't always serve you as a principal. Growth requires letting go of old patterns and choosing new ones. These shifts take intention, but they change everything about how you lead.

From Perfection to Progress

You will make mistakes. You will say the wrong thing in a meeting. You will misread a situation. You will wish you had handled something differently. Mistakes are part of learning. Progress requires reflection, adjustment, and the courage to keep moving forward. The leaders who thrive aren't the ones who never fail. They're the ones who learn from failure and keep going.

From Reactive to Strategic

Most of your day will try to pull you into crisis mode. Emails demand immediate responses. Problems show up unannounced. The urgent drowns out the important. Strategic leaders protect time for what matters most. They create boundaries around their calendars and their energy. They delegate what others can handle. They say no to good things so they can say yes to the right things. This shift from constant reaction to intentional action keeps you focused on the work that moves your school forward.

From Isolation to Connection

Leadership can feel lonely, but you don't have to isolate yourself. You need people who understand the work. You need mentors who've walked the path ahead of you. You need peers who are navigating the same challenges. Connection keeps you grounded and reminds you you're not alone. The strongest leaders build networks of support that sustain them through the hardest seasons.

From Doing to Leading

You were probably promoted because you were great at your job. You solved problems. You got results. But leadership requires a different approach. Your job now is to develop others who solve problems and get results. You multiply impact by building capacity in your people, not by doing their work for them. This shift from being the doer to being the developer is one of the most challenging transitions in leadership, but it's essential for sustainable success.

From External Validation to Internal Conviction

You will not always be appreciated. There will be days when parents complain, teachers resist, and the work feels thankless. If your sense of worth depends on external approval, leadership will exhaust you. Anchor yourself in purpose. Know why you do this work. Let that conviction carry you through the seasons when gratitude is scarce. The leaders who last are the ones who lead from deep conviction, not for applause.

> Anchor yourself in purpose. Know why you do this work. Let that conviction carry you through the seasons when gratitude is scarce.

Your Unique Gifts Matter

You bring something to this work that no one else can. Maybe you see potential in struggling students. Maybe you build trust with skeptical parents. Maybe you turn complex ideas into clear direction. Maybe you bring calm to chaos or energy to stagnation.

Whatever it is, it matters.

Your school needs the leader that only you can be. The one who leads from conviction, not comparison. The one who builds systems that reflect your values. The one who shows up fully, even when it's hard.

Stop waiting to become the leader you think you should be. Start leading as the person you already are.

Addressing the Voices That Hold You Back

If you've ever felt like an imposter, you're not alone. Most leaders wrestle with that voice at some point. It whispers that you don't belong. That you're not qualified. That someone will eventually figure out you don't have it all together. No one has it all together. The leaders you admire are also figuring it out as they go. They've just learned to quiet the doubt long enough to keep moving.

Imposter syndrome grows stronger in isolation. When you bring it into the open, its grip weakens. Start a conversation with a mentor or share your thoughts with a trusted colleague. You'll often discover that your struggles are shared, self-doubt loses its hold, and confidence grows.

You were not accidentally placed in this role. You were called to it. Chosen for it. Equipped for it. The fact that you feel the weight of it means you understand what's at stake. That awareness makes you the right person for the job.

Leading from a Place of Strength

You don't have to be strong in every area. You just have to know where your strengths lie and build a team that complements them.

If you're a visionary but struggle with details, surround yourself with people who excel at execution. If you're great with systems but relationships don't come naturally, invest in leaders who connect deeply with people. If you thrive in strategy but avoid conflict, develop skills or partner with someone who

> Leaders who know their strengths, own their limitations, and strategically build teams around their weaknesses create schools that thrive.

navigates hard conversations well.

Leaders who know their strengths, own their limitations, and strategically build teams around their weaknesses create schools that thrive. Your honesty about your limitations creates space for others to lead. It builds trust. It models the kind of humility that makes schools thrive.

The Work Only You Can Do

There are tasks anyone can do, and then there is the work only you can do. Your effectiveness depends on recognizing this distinction and committing your energy to the work that only you can do, while strategically delegating the rest.

The principal uniquely sets the school's tone and protects its mission amid distractions. They hold the final authority on critical decisions and exemplify leadership through integrity, clarity, and purpose. While principals collaborate widely, these core responsibilities define their irreplaceable role in shaping school culture, guiding instruction, and sustaining progress.

Everything else can and should be delegated, shared, or eliminated. Too many leaders burn out trying to do it all. Protect your time for what matters most. Guard your energy for the decisions and relationships that require your presence. Trust your people to handle the rest.

> Protect your time for what matters most. Guard your energy for the decisions and relationships that require your presence. Trust your people to handle the rest.

You Were Made for This

Your influence reaches further than you can see. Every decision ripples outward. Every conversation shapes someone's experience. The way you lead affects how teachers show up. How teachers show up affects how students learn.

You were created on purpose and for a purpose. You have gifts and talents that only you possess. The world needs you. Your school needs you. Your students need you.

You have what it takes to lead well. You've learned the framework. You've seen how the foundation and pillars work together. You understand the cycle that keeps it all alive.

Now let's bring it all together. The Conclusion will show you how everything you've learned connects to the leader you're becoming and the school you're building. Don't skip it. This is where the pieces come together, and the path forward becomes clear.

Bringing the Dream to Life

This book began with a promise: that purpose-driven leadership is achievable. That finding focus in the chaos is possible. That the thriving school you once dreamed of is within reach.

 Purpose driven leadership is achievable.

Throughout these pages, you've been introduced to a framework built on the purpose foundation and four essential pillars.

Purpose anchors your decisions. It reminds you what matters when the priorities compete. Purpose-centered leaders ask simple questions before they act: Does this move us closer to our mission? Does this serve students and teachers well? Keeping purpose at the forefront ensures that time and energy are directed toward what truly matters.

People give that purpose life. A school's success is carried on the strength of its relationships. Trust is built when words and actions align. Clarity builds when communication is direct and kind. When people feel seen and valued, they contribute with commitment instead of compliance. Strong culture grows from shared respect, not programs.

Pedagogy keeps the focus on learning. It is how purpose reaches the classroom. Leaders who stay close to instruction help teachers connect their daily work to the larger mission. They provide feedback that is both specific and actionable. They identify and acknowledge successes. When teaching aligns with purpose, student achievement rises. Students learn with confidence and curiosity because the classroom provides clear, consistent direction.

Processes bring order and direction to the work. Clear processes enable teams to work toward shared goals, support teacher growth, and foster trust through transparency. When the steps for decision making, feedback, and follow-through are understood, people spend less time reacting and more time creating. Strong processes make change sustainable and keep progress steady long after the initiative begins.

Professional Growth is essential for every school leader. It keeps leadership skills sharp and perspective fresh as education continues to change. When leaders continue to learn, they model curiosity and growth for their staff, setting the tone for a culture that values continuous improvement. Prioritizing your own development strengthens your ability to guide others, support collaboration, and build morale. As everyone grows together, teaching improves, students benefit, and the entire school moves forward with shared purpose.

The purpose foundation and four pillars create the structure. The Assess-Design-Align cycle keeps them strong. The cycle is a continuous process that helps you identify needs, create targeted solutions, and coordinate efforts to achieve lasting, aligned improvement.

Assess to understand what is true. Look at culture, systems, assessments, instruction, and people. Listen before deciding. Establish feedback loops with every stakeholder, from teachers to students to families, to gain a comprehensive understanding of how the school is functioning. This kind of assessment turns information into insight and guides where to focus next.

Design a plan that balances what is working and what needs attention. Use what was learned during assessment to determine how the school will celebrate strengths, reinforce effective practices, and address weaknesses with clear strategies and support. This stage turns understanding into direction, making progress intentional.

Align every part of the work back to its purpose. Ensure that decisions, systems, and actions still reflect the mission and values that guide the school. Alignment keeps improvement from drifting and brings stability to growth. When purpose stays at the center, the work moves in a clear direction, and the results last.

Repeating the cycle builds efficiency and confidence. With each round, leaders make decisions faster and with greater accuracy, using less mental energy. Familiar routines prevent fatigue, reveal patterns more quickly, and maintain consistent work over time.

But frameworks are only as powerful as the leaders who use them.

The transformation doesn't happen because you read this book. It happens because you choose to lead differently. It happens when you stop reacting and start designing, when you stop guessing and start assessing, and when you stop drifting and start aligning. It happens when you decide that your school will reflect the vision you once held, and you commit to doing the work required to make it happen.

That work won't always be easy. There will be days when you question whether it's worth it. Days when the resistance feels overwhelming. Days when you wonder if anything you're doing actually matters.

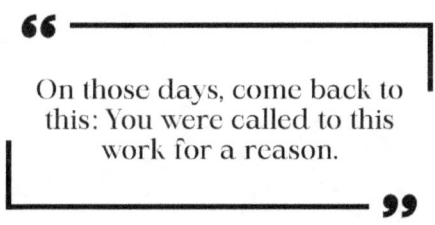

On those days, come back to this: You were called to this work for a reason.

On those days, come back to this: You were called to this work for a reason.

Not because you're perfect, but because you're willing. Not because you have all the answers, but because you're brave enough to ask the right questions. Not because the work is easy, but because the work is worth it.

Lead with integrity when it costs you something. Lead with courage when the outcome is uncertain. Lead with purpose when everything else pulls you off course.

Your school is waiting. Your teachers are watching. Your students are counting on you.

Now go and lead with purpose. Be the leader you were created to be.

From the Author

This book came from years of leading, failing, learning, and trying again. I wrote it because I've sat where you're sitting: behind a desk late at night with a mountain of work and no one to call. I've felt the weight of wanting desperately to make a difference, yet feeling paralyzed about where to begin. Not because the ideas weren't there, but because everything felt urgent and there was never enough time.

The Purpose-Driven Principal came from realizing I had a purpose and could help others find theirs. When we started filtering everything (meetings, programs, decisions, roles, expectations) by asking why we were doing it, what purpose it served, and how it helped us accomplish our mission, my leadership transformed. I watched that transformation ripple through my staff as they discovered and began living out their own purposes. We stopped just surviving and started creating the school we'd always dreamed of, where teachers led joyfully from their strengths, students recognized their unique gifts, and purpose shaped every decision we made.

If this book helped you see your next step more clearly, I'm grateful. If it helped you figure out where to put your time and what to let go of, even better.

If you're reading this and still feel stuck, know that I've been there too. The work is hard, and it doesn't get easier. But it does get clearer when you know what you're building toward. Every principal needs a coach, someone who's been in the seat and can help you sort through what matters most. If you'd like to continue this conversation, I'd love to connect. Visit sloanleadership.com to learn more about coaching, school consulting, and leadership development.

Thank you for the work you do every day.

~Michelle

About the Author

Michelle Sloan is an educational consultant with over 25 years in education as an elementary educator and principal. As founder of Sloan Leadership Solutions, Michelle works with school leaders across public, private, and charter schools internationally. She provides coaching and mentorship to new principals, helping them succeed from day one. She also partners with existing schools to develop strategic plans, realign mission and vision, and get back on track toward excellence. Michelle delivers transformational professional development through collaborative cohorts. Her heart is helping leaders discover their God-given gifts and talents, then guiding them to make their dreams come alive. She believes everyone has a purpose, and when leaders live it out on purpose, they create a transformative impact on the world around them.

Contact Michelle Sloan
Email: msloan@sloanleadership.com
FB: @sloanleadershipsolutions
IG: @sloanleadership

References

Adelman, H. S., & Taylor, L. (2019). Improving school improvement. Center for Mental Health in Schools & Student/Learning Supports at UCLA. https://smhp.psych.ucla.edu/pdfdocs/WINTER25.pdf

Alsubaie, M. A. (2024). Resource inadequacy as a barrier to effective curriculum implementation: Challenges and strategies. International Journal of Academic and Applied Studies, 12(1). https://files.eric.ed.gov/fulltext/EJ1430070.pdf

Balfanz, R., Bridgeland, J., Fox, J. H., DePaoli, J. L., Ingram, E. S., & Maushard, M. (2024). Building a culture of belonging in schools. Johns Hopkins University, Everyone Graduates Center.

Bauer, S. C., Thomas, C., & Bowers, A. J. (2021). Principal well-being and the challenges of school leadership. Educational Administration Quarterly, 57(3), 389–420.

Boothe, A. (2024). The model classroom approach: Promoting inquiry in every classroom. Principal Principles.

Bryk, A. S., & Schneider, B. (2002). Trust in schools: A core resource for improvement. Russell Sage Foundation.

CASEL. (2024). State of social and emotional learning in schools: Annual report 2024. Collaborative for Academic, Social, and Emotional Learning.

Chapman, G., & White, P. (2019). The 5 languages of appreciation in the workplace: Empowering organizations by encouraging people (Updated ed.). Northfield Publishing.

Clear, J. (2018). Atomic habits: An easy & proven way to build good habits & break bad ones. Avery.

Coe, R., Aloisi, C., Higgins, S., & Major, L. E. (2014). What makes great teaching? Sutton Trust.

Darling-Hammond, L., Hyler, M. E., & Gardner, M. (2017). Effective teacher professional development. Learning Policy Institute.

District Administration. (2024). The benefits of teacher collaboration. District Administration. https://districtadministration.com/article/the-benefits-of-teacher-collaboration/

DuFour, R., & DuFour, R. (2019). Professional learning communities at work: Best practices for enhancing student achievement (3rd ed.). Solution Tree Press.

Economic Policy Institute. (2019). The teacher shortage is real, large, and growing, and worse than we thought.

Forman, S. G., Shapiro, E. S., Codding, R. S., Gonzales, J. E., Reddy, L. A., Rosenfield, S. A., Sanetti, L. M. H., & Stoiber, K. C. (2019). Implementation science and school psychology. School Psychology, 34(5), 483–496.

Frontline Education. (2025). The impact of personalized professional learning on teacher retention. Frontline Research & Learning Institute.

Gallup. (2020). State of the American workplace: Employee engagement insights. Gallup Press.

George, B., & Sims, P. (2007). True north: Discover your authentic leadership. Jossey-Bass.

Gordon, J., & Kelly, A. P. (2024). Difficult conversations don't have to be difficult: A simple, smart way to make your relationships and team better. Wiley.

Gordon, J., & West, D. (2019). The coffee bean: A simple lesson to create positive change. Wiley.

Greater Good Science Center. (2025). Purpose. University of California, Berkeley. https://greatergood.berkeley.edu/topic/purpose

Hamre, B. K., & Pianta, R. C. (2001). Early teacher–child relationships and the trajectory of children's school outcomes through eighth grade. Child Development, 72(2), 625–638.

Hattie, J. (2008). Visible learning: A synthesis of over 800 meta-analyses relating to achievement. Routledge.

Hewson, K., & Hewson, L. (2022). Collaborative response: The three foundational components that transform how we respond to the needs of learners. Jigsaw Learning.

Institute of Education Sciences. (2025). Continuous improvement in education: A toolkit for schools and districts. U.S. Department of

Education. https://ies.ed.gov/ies/2025/01/continuous-improvement-education-toolkit-schools-and-districts

Kopp, W. (2011). A Chance to Make History: What Works and What Doesn't in Providing an Excellent Education for All. PublicAffairs.

Lane, J. (2023). Clarity, connection, momentum: An ebook for educators [Ebook]. Jessica Lane Consulting. https://www.data-informedimpact.com/

Learning Forward, & Wallace Foundation. (2021). The role of the principal in leading learning: Insights from research.

Learning Policy Institute. (2017). The positive impact of professional development on teacher retention.

Lencioni, P. (2004). Death by meeting: A leadership fable...about solving the most painful problem in business. Jossey-Bass.

Maxwell, John C. Developing the Leader Within You. Thomas Nelson, 1993.

Maxwell, J. C. (n.d.). The Maxwell leadership Bible (3rd ed.). Thomas Nelson.

McConnell, J. C. (2019). WIN Time: What I need—Closing the gap between teaching and learning. JMC Publications.

National Center for Education Statistics. (2023). Principal turnover: Findings from the principal follow-up survey 2023. U.S. Department of Education.

Ratatouille. Directed by Brad Bird and Jan Pinkava, Buena Vista Pictures, 2007.

Rath, T., & Conchie, B. (2008). Strengths-based leadership: Great leaders, teams, and why people follow. Gallup Press.

Roorda, D. L., Koomen, H. M. Y., Spilt, J. L., & Oort, F. J. (2011). The influence of affective teacher–student relationships on students' school engagement and achievement: A meta-analytic approach. Review of Educational Research, 81(4), 493–529.

RTI International. (2023). How leadership influences student learning: A review of research. Wallace Foundation. https://wallacefoundation.org/sites/default/files/2023-07/How-Leadership-Influences-Student-Learning.pdf

Shackleton, E. H. (1919). South: The story of Shackleton's last expedition 1914-1917. William Heinemann.

Sinek, S (2011) Start with why: How great leaders inspire everyone to take action. Portfolio/Penguin.

Watts, C. (2025). The Craft of Clarity. Principal Principles.